MATHEMATICS
LAB MANUAL
CLASS-IX

A Complete Lab Activity Book

Authors

Mr. Rohit Manglik
(N.I.T, Surathkal)

Mr. Mohit Tripathi
(M.Sc., B.Ed.)

Strictly according to the latest syllabus prescribed by

Central Board of Secondary Education (CBSE)

And

State Boards of Chhattisgarh, Haryana, Bihar, Jharkhand, Kerala, Mizoram,

Meghalaya, and other states following the CBSE curriculum

Title	: Mathematics Lab Manual - IX
Author Name	: Mr. Rohit Manglik, Mr. Mohit Tripathi
Published By	: EduGorilla Community Pvt. Ltd.
Publishers Address	: 12/651, First Floor Opp. Arvindo Park, Near Jama Masjid, Indira Nagar, Lucknow, Uttar Pradesh - 226016, India

Copyright

Disclaimer

<u>PREFACE</u>

With the NEP 2020 and expansion of research and knowledge has changed the face of education to a great extent. In the Modern times, education is not just constricted top the lecture method but also includes a practical knowledge of certain subjects. This way of education helps a student to grasp the basic concepts and principles. Thus, trying to break the stereotype that subjects like Mathematics, and Science means studying lengthy formulas, complex structures, and handling complicated instruments, we are trying to make education easy, fun, and enjoyable.

The new CBSE syllabus for Mathematics, which help in comprehension of concepts and try to develop the scientific attitude and basic laboratory skills desired at this level.

The present book Mathematics Lab Manual Class IX has been written to meet the requirements of new curriculum in the practical work for class 9 following NEP 2020.

The purpose of this manual is not only to convey the approach of the laboratory courses but also to provide the students appropriate guidance required for carrying out the experiments in science laboratories. All the experiments in this manual have been given to conform a systematic format that includes Aim, Theory, Material Required, Procedure, Observation, Result, Precautions, Viva-Voce and Suggested Activities.

The Theory given with each experiment is a very special feature of this lab manual. It gives the complete understanding of each Concept/Term & Definition etc. so that students need not to refer their textbooks or any other book. Viva-Voce questions given with each experiment aims to test a student's understanding of the related experiment. To provide the student a basic idea of investigatory projects, some investigatory projects have been included as well.

<u>SOME SPECIAL FEATURES</u>

- Detailed and step-by-step procedure for each experiment.
- Viva-voce questions been designed to have grasp on the skill & knowledge required for an experiment
- Clearly labelled diagrams demonstrate the correct way of handling laboratory apparatus and pert the experiments methodically.

CONTENT

ACTIVITY 1

OBJECTIVE

To represent an irrational number on the number line.
(To represent $\sqrt{2}$ on a number line).

MATERIAL REQUIRED

A sheet of white paper, pencil, compass, eraser and ruler etc.

THEORY

Pythagoras theorem:

In a right-angled triangle, the square of the hypotenuse is equal to the sum of the squares of the other two sides containing a right angle.

In a right-angled triangle, if the base and perpendicular are of 1 unit each, the hypotenuse will be $\sqrt{(1^2 + 1^2)} = \sqrt{2}$.

Now, by using this concept, we will represent $\sqrt{2}$ on the number line.

PROCEDURE

1. Draw a line X'OX. on the white sheet.
2. Divide the line into equal parts from point O by paper folding activity taking each part as 1 unit. Mark the points as 1,2,3 .... etc.
3. Draw the perpendicular at the point marked as '1' by paper folding.
4. Unfold the paper and draw the line at the crease so formed.
5. Mark a point A on this crease at 1 unit from line X'OX.
6. Join O and A, we get $OA = \sqrt{2}$ units. (By Pythagoras theorem)
7. Take O as a centre, OA as radius, draw an arc intersecting the line X'OX at M.

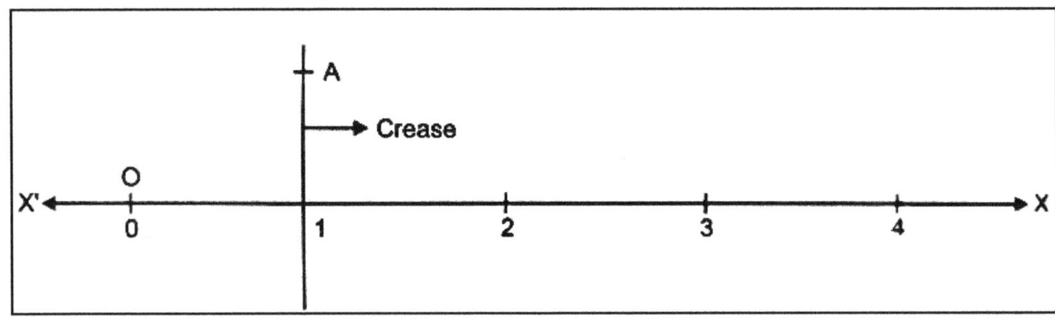

OBSERVATION

We observe that $OA = OM = \sqrt{2}$ units.

RESULT

An irrational number $\sqrt{2}$ is represented on the number line.

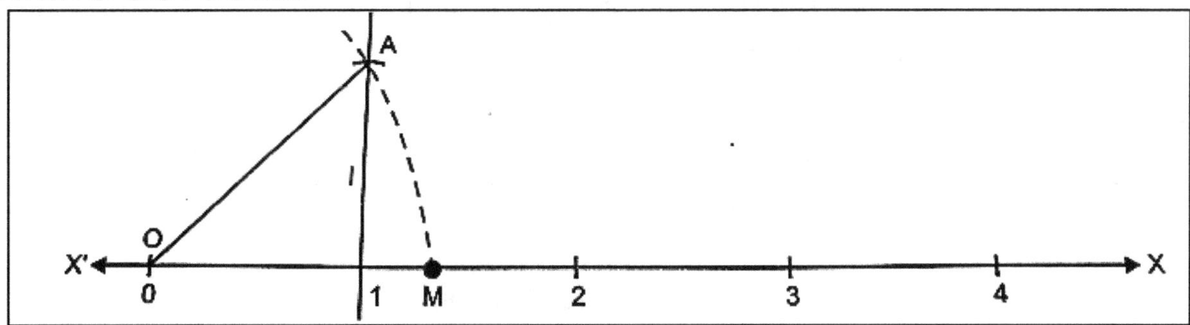

Students can represent any irrational number on a number line by using the above method.

e.g., $(\sqrt{3})^2 = (\sqrt{2})^2 + (1)^2$

At M, by paper folding draw perpendicular BM on the number line of 1 unit. Join OB. With O as centre and OB as radius draw an arc intersecting the line at N.

Thus $OB = ON = \sqrt{3}$ on the number line.

ACTIVITY TIME

Represent other irrational numbers such as $\sqrt{3}, \sqrt{5}, \sqrt{7}$ ..., etc., on the number line

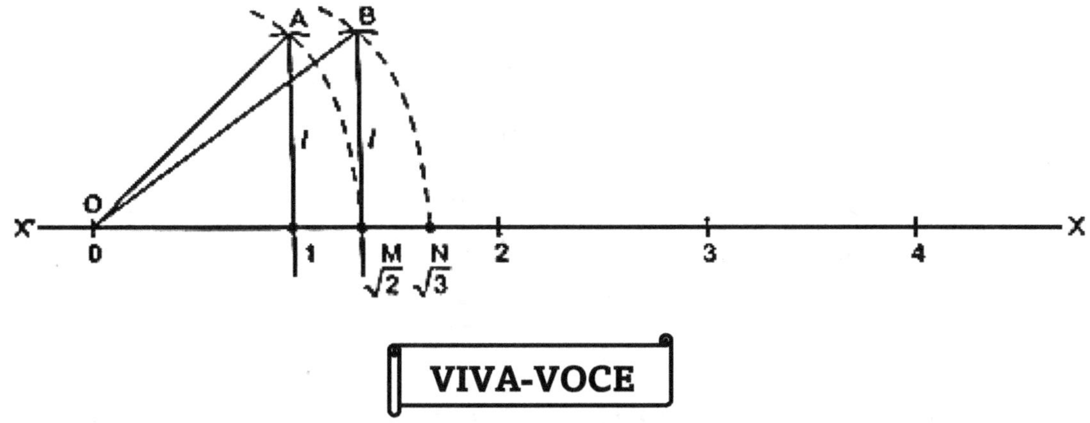

VIVA-VOCE

Question 1. Is every irrational number, a real number?
Answer: Yes, because real numbers consist of both rational and irrational numbers.

Question 2. Does the square roots of all positive integers, irrational? Give reason.
Answer: No, square roots of all positive integers are not irrational, e.g., $S = \sqrt{9} = 3^2$, which is a rational number.

Question 3. "Sum of two irrational numbers is an irrational number". Is this statement true?
Answer: No, it's not true, the sum of two irrational numbers may be irrational or rational.

Question 4. Can we apply Pythagoras theorem in any triangle?
Answer: No, Pythagoras theorem is applicable only in the right-angled triangles.

Question 5. How would you find a base of a right-angled triangle, if hypotenuse and perpendicular are given?
Answer: Base $= \sqrt{(\text{hypotenuse})^2 - (\text{perpendicular})^2}$

Question 6. Is it possible that the sum of two irrational numbers can be represented on number line?
Answer: Yes.

Question 1.
From the choices given below mark the co-prime numbers:
(a) 2,3
(b) 2,4
(c) 2,6
(d) 2,10

Question 2.
A rational number equivalent to $\frac{5}{7}$ is:
(a) $\frac{15}{17}$
(b) $\frac{25}{27}$
(c) $\frac{10}{14}$
(d) $\frac{10}{27}$

Question 3.
An example of a whole number is:
(a) 0
(b) $-\frac{1}{2}$
(c) $\frac{11}{5}$
(c) -7

Question 4.
Given a rational number $-\frac{5}{9}$. This rational number can also be known as:
(a) A natural number
(b) A whole number
(c) A fraction
(d) A real number

Question 5.
The rational number $0.\overline{3}$ can also be written as:
(a) 0.3
(b) $\frac{3}{10}$
(c) 0.33
(d) $\frac{1}{3}$

Question 6.
If the decimal representation of a number is non-terminating, non-repeating then the number is:
(a) A natural number
(b) A rational number
(c) A whole number
(d) An irrational number

Question 7.
The square root of which number is rational:
(a) 7
(b) 1.96
(c) 0.04
(d) 13

Question 8.
A rational number between $\frac{1}{7}$ and $\frac{2}{7}$ is:
(a) $\frac{10}{21}$
(b) $\frac{2}{21}$
(c) $\frac{5}{14}$
(d) $\frac{5}{21}$

Question 9.
The number 1.101001000100001... is:
(a) A natural number
(b) A whole number
(c) A rational number
(d) An irrational number

Question 10.
On adding $2\sqrt{3}$ and $3\sqrt{2}$ we get:
(a) $5\sqrt{5}$
(b) $5(\sqrt{3} + \sqrt{2})$
(c) $2\sqrt{3} + 3\sqrt{2}$
(d) None of these

ANSWER KEY

1.(a)	2.(c)	3.(a)	4.(d)	5.(d)	6.(d)	7.(b)	8.(d)	9.(d)	10.(c)

OBJECTIVE

To make a square root spiral by using paper folding.

MATERIAL REQUIRED

Tracing paper, pencil, geometry box.

THEORY

In a right-angled triangle, the square of the hypotenuse is equal to the sum of the squares of the other two sides.

e.g., $\sqrt{2} = \sqrt{(1^2 + 1^2)}$. By using this Concept, we will represent irrational numbers on a number line by paper folding.

PROCEDURE

To represent $\sqrt{2}$ on a number line.

1. Draw a line OX on the tracing paper. Mark point O on one end and mark point 0,1,2, 3, … at equal distances of 1 unit by paper folding.

2. Fold the paper along the line that passes through the point marked '1' and perpendicular to the line OX, i.e., fold the paper in such a way that point 'O' coincides with point '2'. Make a crease and unfold it. From the point marked '1', draw a line of length 1 unit moving along the crease. Mark the point as M such that PM =1 unit. Join OM, clearly OM = $\sqrt{2}$ units.

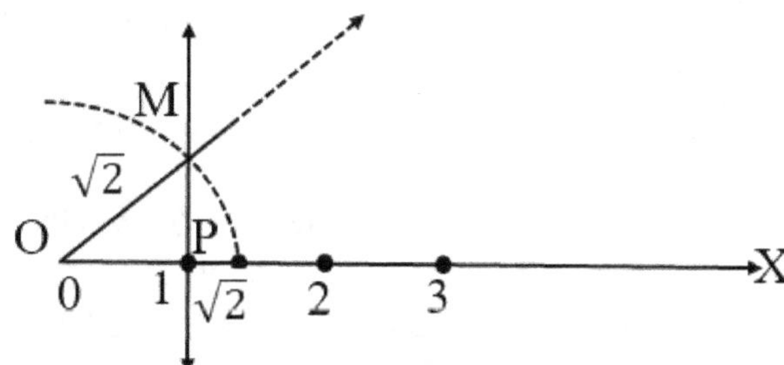

3. Fold the paper along the line (fold on point M in such a way that point O joined with any point

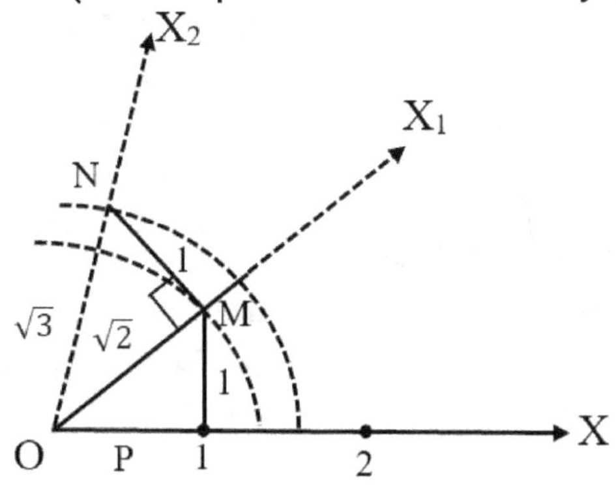

lie on OX₁) that passes through point M and perpendicular to OM at M. Make a crease and unfold it. From the point, M, draw a line of 1 unit moving upward, along the crease. Mark the point as N such that MN = 1 unit. Join ON, where $ON = \sqrt{3}$. Keep this process continues to get $\sqrt{4}, \sqrt{5}, \sqrt{6}, \ldots \ldots \ldots$

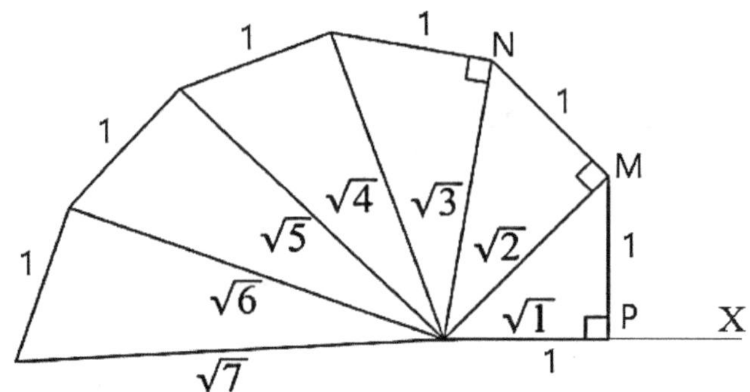

RESULT

In this way, we get a square root spiral pattern by using paper folding.

LEARNING OUTCOME

On the same plane, different irrational numbers can be represented on the number line by paper folding method.

By using Pythagoras' theorem students will be able to construct a square root spiral by paper folding method.

ACTIVITY TIME

Represent square root of 7 and 9 by constructing a square root spiral.

VIVA-VOCE

Question 1. Define a rational number.
Answer: A number that can be expressed in the form of p/q, where q ≠ 0 and p, q are integers, is called a rational number.

Question 2. Define an irrational number.
Answer: A number that cannot be expressed in the form of p/q, where $q \neq 0$ and p, q are integers, is called an irrational number.

Question 3. Define a real number.
Answer: A number that may be either rational or irrational is called a real number.

Question 4. How many rational and irrational numbers lie between any two real numbers?
Answer: There are infinite rational and irrational numbers that lie between any two real numbers.

Question 5. In which triangle, Pythagoras theorem is applicable?
Answer: Right-angled triangle.

Question 6. Give some examples of irrational numbers.
Answer: Some examples of irrational numbers are $\sqrt{5}, 3 - \sqrt{7}, 2\pi$ etc.

Question 7. Can we represent the reciprocal of zero on the number line.
Answer: No, because reciprocal of zero is an undefined term, so we cannot represent it on the number line.

Question 8. Is it possible that we make a square root spiral of negative numbers?
Answer: No.

Question 1:

A rational number between $\frac{-2}{3}$ and $\frac{3}{2}$ is:

(a) $\frac{12}{5}$

(b) $\frac{5}{12}$

(c) $\frac{-4}{5}$

(d) $\frac{5}{4}$

Question 2:

The simplest form of a rational number $\frac{177}{413}$ is:

(a) $\frac{7}{13}$

(b) $\frac{2}{59}$

(c) $\frac{3}{7}$

(d) $\frac{3}{5}$

Question 3.

The vulgar fraction of $3.\overline{13}$ is given by:

(a) $\frac{99}{310}$

(b) $\frac{310}{99}$

(c) $\frac{101}{11}$

(d) $\frac{29}{9}$

Question 4.

The irrational number between 2 and $\sqrt{5}$ is:

(a) $2\sqrt{5}$

(b) $2\sqrt{\sqrt{5}}$

(c) $(10)^{\frac{1}{2}}$

(d) $\sqrt{2\sqrt{5}}$

Question 5.

If m and n are non-negative integers, the denominator of a terminating decimal is of the form:

(a) $2^n \times 3^n$

(b) $3^m \times 5^n$

(c) $2^n \times 3^m$

(d) $2^m \times 5^n$

Question 6.

The product of irrational numbers $5\sqrt{3}$ and $21\sqrt{3}$ is given by:

(a) 325

(b) 315

(c) 335

(d) 345

Question 7.

The difference between a rational number and an irrational number is:

(a) May be a rational number.

(b) Always a rational number.

(c) An irrational number.

(d) An integer.

Question 8.

Rationalization of $\frac{1}{\sqrt{7}-2}$ is:

(a) $\frac{1}{2}\sqrt{7} + \frac{2}{3}$

(b) $\sqrt{7} + \frac{2}{3}$

(c) $\frac{1}{3}\sqrt{7} + \frac{1}{3}$

(d) $\frac{1}{3}\sqrt{7} + \frac{2}{3}$

Question 9.

The simplest form of the expression $\left(\frac{625}{81}\right)^{-1/2}$

(a) $\frac{125}{27}$

(b) $\frac{27}{125}$

(c) $\frac{9}{25}$

(d) $\frac{25}{9}$

Question 10.

The fifth root of 243 is given by:

(a) 9

(b) -9

(c) -3

(d) 3

OBJECTIVE

To verify the identity $(a + b)^2 = a^2 + 2ab + b^2$ by paper cutting and pasting.

MATERIAL REQUIRED

A sheet of white paper, three sheets of glazed paper (different colours), a pair of scissors, glue stick and a geometry box.

THEORY

1. Square and its area.
2. Rectangle and its area.

PROCEDURE

Take distinct values of a and b, say a = 4 units, b = 2 units

1. Cut a square of side a (say 4 units) on a glazed paper (blue).

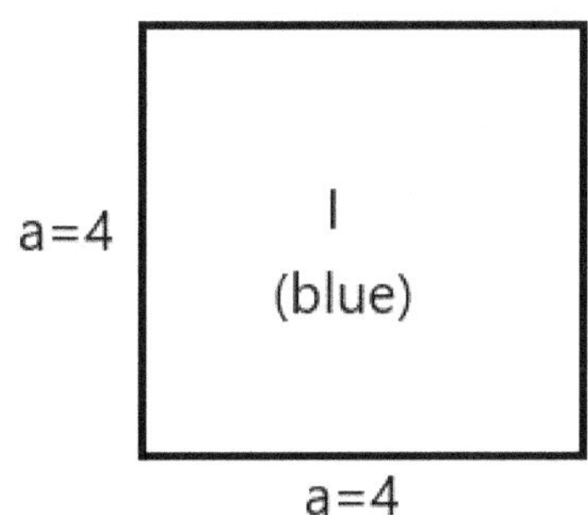

2. Cut a square of side b (say 2 units) on glazed paper (pink).
3. Now, cut two rectangles of length a (4 units) and breadth b (2 units) from the third glazed paper (red).
4. Draw a square PQRS of $(a + b) = (4 + 2)$, 6 units on a white paper sheet as shown in fig. (i).

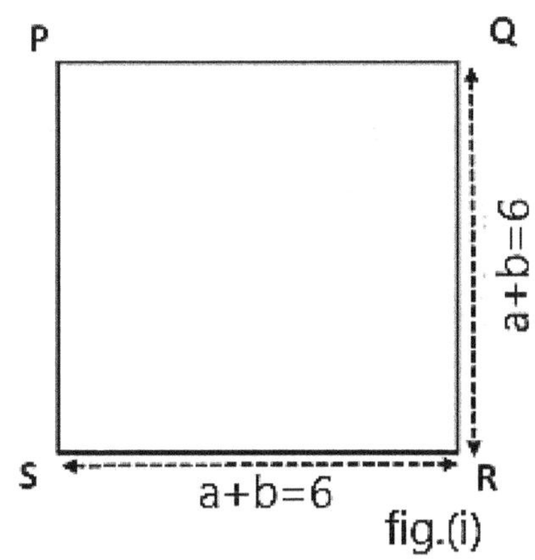

fig.(i)

5. Paste the squares I and II and two rectangles III and IV on the same white squared paper.

6. Arrange all the pieces on the white square sheet in such a way that they form a square ABCD fig. (ii).

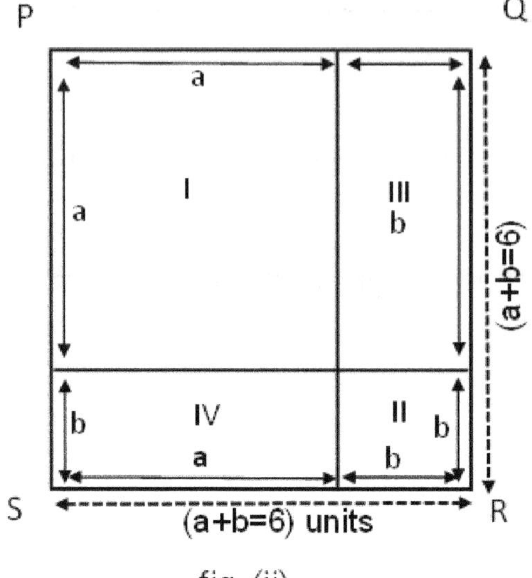

fig. (ii).

OBSERVATION

1. Area of the square PQRS on the white sheet of paper
    $(a + b)^2 = (4 + 2)^2 = 6 \times 6 = 36.$ sq. units..(i)

2. Area of two-coloured squares I and II
    area of Ist square$= a^2 = 4^2 = 16$ sq. units
    area of IInd square$= b^2 = 2^2 = 4$ sq. units

3. Area of two-coloured rectangles III and IV$= 2(a \times b) = 2(4 \times 2) = 16$ sq. units
    Now, total area of four quadrilaterals (calculated)
    $$= a^2 + b^2 + 2(ab)$$
    $$= 16 + 4 + 16$$
    $$= 36 \text{ sq. units } \dots\dots\dots\dots\dots\dots\dots\dots\dots\dots\dots\dots\dots(ii)$$

    Area of square ABCD =Total area of four quadrilaterals = 36 sq. units
    Equating (i) and (ii)
    Area of square PQRS = Area of square ABCD i.e.,
    $$(a + b)^2 = a^2 + b^2 + 2ab$$

RESULT

Algebraic identity $(a + b)^2 = a^2 + b^2 + 2ab$ is verified.

LEARNING OUTCOME

The identity $(a + b)^2 = a^2 + b^2 + 2ab$ is verified by cutting and pasting of paper. This identity can be verified geometrically by taking other values of a and b.

ACTIVITY TIME

Verify this activity by taking
1. $a = 2$ and $b = 3$
2. $a = 6$ and $b = 9$

VIVA-VOCE

Question 1. What do you mean by algebraic expression?

Answer: A combination of constants and variables, connected by four fundamental arithmetic operations $+, -, \times$ and $\div$ is called an algebraic expression.

Question 2. Are $(a + b)^2$ and $a^2 + 2ab + b^2$ algebraic expressions?

Answer: Yes, both $(a + b)^2$ and $a^2 + 2ab + b^2$ are algebraic expressions because they contain both variables (a and b) and arithmetic operations $(+)$.

Question 3. What is the coefficient of x^2 in $(3x + 1)^2$?

Answer: 9.

Question 4. Is the expansion of $(x + y + z)^2$, trinomial?

Answer: No, because on expanding $(x + y + z)^2$, we get six terms.

Question 5. What do you mean by a trinomial?

Answer: A polynomial with three terms is called a trinomial

Question 6. Write the product of $(7x + 3)(7x + 3$.

Answer: $49x^2 + 42x + 9$.

Question 7. What do you mean by a binomial?

Answer: A polynomial with two terms is called a binomial.

MULTIPLE CHOICE QUESTION

Question 1.

The expression $x + 3$ is in

(a) One variable
(b) Two variables
(c) No variable
(d) None of these.

Question 2.

The expression $4xy + 7$ is in

(a) One variable
(b) Two variables
(c) No variable
(d) None of these.

Question 3.

Which of the following is a monomial?

(a) $4x^2$
(b) $a + 6$
(c) $a + 6 + c$
(d) $a + b + c + d$.

Question 4.

Which of the following is a trinomial?

(a) $-7z$
(b) $z^2 - 4y^2$
(c) $x^2y - xy^2 + y^2$
(d) $12a - 9ab + 5b - 3$

Question 5.

The value of $x^2 - 2x + 1$ when $x = 1$ is

(a) 1
(b) 2
(c) -1
(d) 0.

Question 6.

Which of the following is a binomial?

(a) $3xy$
(b) $4l + 5m$
(c) $2x + 3y - 5$
(d) $4a - 7ab + 3b + 12$.

<table>
<tr><td>

Question 7.
Find the factors of $3 + 2\sqrt{3}x + x^2$?
(a) $(x + \sqrt{3})^2$
(b) $(x - \sqrt{3})^2$
(c) $x^2 + 3$
(d) None of these

Question 8.
The expression $4x^2 + 12x + 9$ represents an area of a square, write the dimensions of a square.
(a) $(2x + 3)$ by $(2x + 3)$
(b) $(2x - 3)$ by $(2x + 3)$
(c) $2x + 1$
(d) None of these

</td><td>

Question 9.
If $(a + b)^2 = 25, a^2 = 4, 2ab = 12$, then what will be the value of a and b?
(a) $a = -2, b = 3$
(b) $a = 2, b = -3$
(c) $a = 2, b = 3$
(d) None of these

Question 10.
Write the factors of $169 + 26y + y^2$
(a) $(y - 13)^2$
(b) $(13 + y)^2$
(c) $(13 - y)^2$
(d) None of these

</td></tr>
</table>

Answer Key

| 1.(a) | 2.(b) | 3.(a) | 4.(c) | 5.(d) | 6.(b) | 7.(a) | 8.(a) | 9.(c) | 10.(b) |

ACTIVITY 4

ALGEBRAIC IDENTITY
$(a - b)^2 = a^2 - 2ab + b^2$

OBJECTIVE
To verify the identity $(a - b)^2 = (a^2 - 2ab + b^2)$ by paper cutting and pasting.

MATERIAL REQUIRED
Drawing sheet, pencil, coloured paper, scissors, ruler, glue.

THEORY
1. Square and its area.
2. Rectangle and its area.

PROCEDURE
Take two distinct values of a and b, say $a = 7$ units and $b = 3$ units.
1. Draw a square I of side a (say 7 units) on the white sheet of paper, fill with red colour and name it as AHEI, fig. (i).
2. Find the value of $a - b$, i.e., $7 - 3 = 4$ units.
3. Now, draw two rectangles II and III each having length $(a - b)$, i.e., $7 - 3 = 4$ units and breadth b = units, on a pink glazed paper, fig. (ii).
4. Draw a square IV of side $b = 3$ units on a different glazed paper, say,blue, fig. (iii).

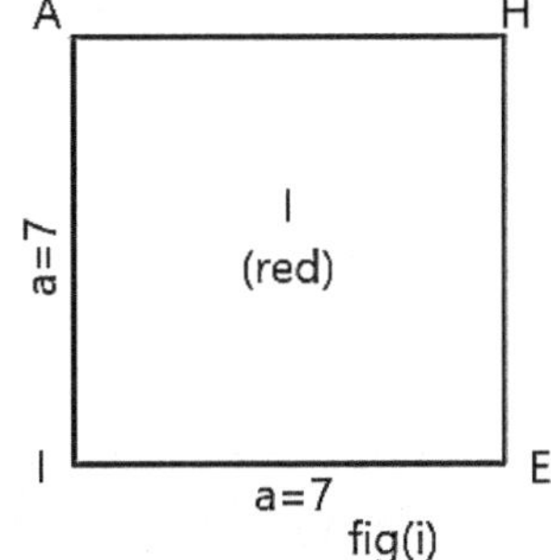

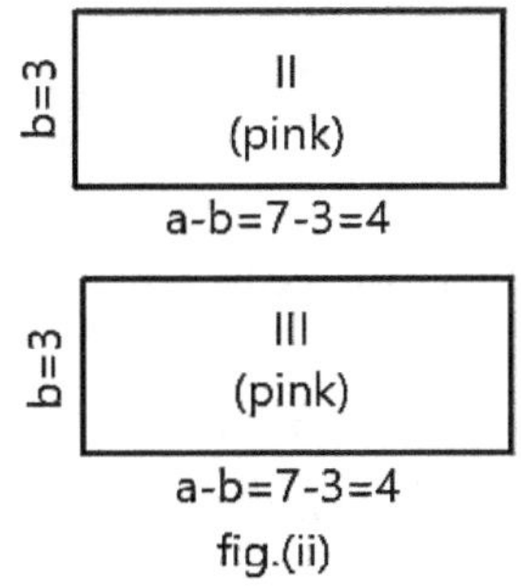

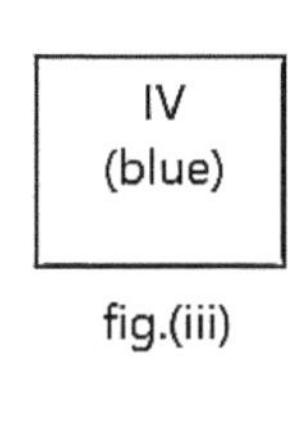

5. Now, cut rectangles II and III and square IV from glazed papers and paste them on a white sheet of paper. Arrange all these pieces inside the square AHIE as shown in fig.(iv).

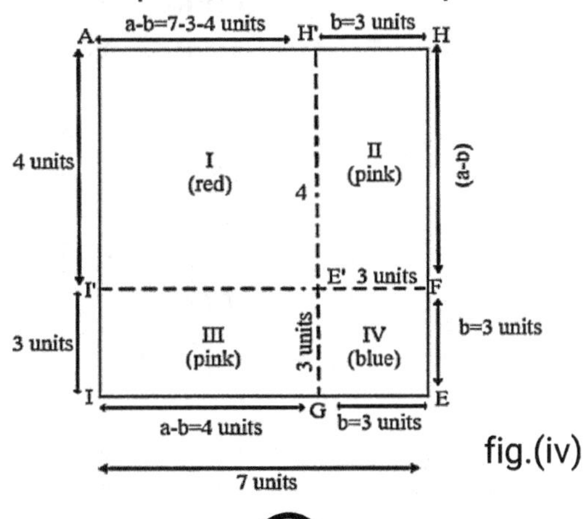

OBSERVATION

After pasting three strips, a red portion is left for measurement, i.e., $(a - b)$ by $(a - b)$ which is a square AH'E'I'.

$$\text{Area of square AH'E'I'} = (a - b)(a - b) = (a - b)^2 = 4 \times 4 = 4^2 = 16 \text{ sq. units}$$
$$\text{Area of square AHEI} = a^2 = (7)^2 = 49 \text{ sq. units}$$

Or we can say that,

$$\text{Area of square AH'E'I'} = \text{Area of square AHEI} - (\text{Area of three pieces II, III and IV}).$$

Now, the area of two rectangles II and III $= 2 \times b(a - b)$
$$= 2 \times 3 \times 4 = 24 \text{ sq. units}$$
$$\text{Area of square IV} = b^2 = (3)^2 = 9 \text{ sq. units}$$
$$\text{Area of square AH'E'I'} = a^2 - [2ab - 2b^2 + b^2]$$
$$= (a - b)^2 = a^2 - 2ab + b^2$$
$$= 49 - 2 \times 7 \times 3 + 9$$
$$= 49 - 42 + 9$$
$$= 16 \text{ sq. units}$$

RESULT

Algebraic Identity $(a - b)^2 = a^2 - 2ab + b^2$ is verified.

LEARNING OUTCOME

In this way, we can verify the identity $(a - b)^2 = a^2 - 2ab + b^2$ geometrically.

ACTIVITY TIME

Verify the algebraic identity $(a - b)^2 = a^2 - 2ab + b^2$ by taking $a = 9$ and $b = 4$.

VIVA-VOCE

Question 1: What do you mean by an algebraic identity?
Answer: An algebraic identity is an algebraic equation that is true for all values of variables occurring in it.

Question 2: Is $(x - 3y)^2 = x^2 - 6xy + 9y^2$ an algebraic identity?
Answer: Yes.

Question 3: Which identity should be used to expand $(3x - 2y)^2$?
Answer: $(a - b)^2 = a^2 - 2ab + b^2$

Question 4: The algebraic identity is true for every real number.
Answer: Yes.

Question 5. Write general quadratic polynomial's.
Answer: $ax^2 + bx + c$, where $a \neq 0$

Question 6: Suppose we want a square of any natural number, then it is possible to find the square of any natural number by using the identity $(a - b)^2 = a^2 + b^2 - 2ab$.
Answer: Yes.

Question 7: What do we mean by the degree of an algebraic expression?
Answer: The highest power of the variable involved in the algebraic expression is called its degree.

Question 1.
Which of the following is the numerical coefficient of x^2y^2?
(a) 0
(b) 1
(c) x^2
(d) y^2

Question 2.
Which of the following is the numerical coefficient of $-5xy$?
(a) 5
(b) $-x$
(c) -5
(d) $-y$

Question 3.
Which of the following is obtained by subtracting $x^2 - y^2$ from $y^2 - x^2$?
(a) $2(x^2 - y^2)$
(b) $-2(x^2 + y^2)$
(c) $2(x^2 + y^2)$
(d) $2(x^2 - y^2)$

Question 4.
The value of $x^2 - 5$ at $x = -1$ is
(a) -2
(b) -1
(c) -4
(d) -5

Question 5.
$a^2 - b^2$ is a product of
(a) $(a + b)(a - b)$
(b) $(a + b)(a + b)$
(c) $(a - b)(a - b)$
(d) None of these

Question 6.
Which of the following is the value of $\left(x + \frac{1}{x}\right)^2$?
(a) $x^2 + \frac{1}{x^2}$
(b) $x^2 - \frac{1}{x^2}$
(c) $x^2 + \frac{1}{x^2} + 2$
(d) $x^2 + \frac{1}{x^2} + 2x$

Question 7.
pqr is what type of polynomial?
(a) Monomial
(b) Binomial
(c) Trinomial
(d) None of these

Question 8.
What degree does $x^3 - x^2y^2 - 8y^2 + 2$ have?
(a) 2
(b) 3
(c) 4
(d) 7

Question 9.
What is the value of $5x^{25} - 3x^{32} + 2x^{-12}$ at $x = 1$?
(a) 0
(b) 2
(c) 4
(d) None of these

Question 10.
What is the product of $(x + a)$ and $(x + b)$?
(a) $x^2 + (a - b)x + ab$
(b) $x^2 + (a + b)x - ab$
(c) $x^2 + (a + b)x - ab$
(d) $x^2 + (a + b)x + ab$

ANSWER KEY

1.(b)	2.(c)	3.(a)	4.(c)	5.(a)	6.(c)	7.(a)	8.(c)	9.(c)	10.(a)

OBJECTIVE
Learning geometrical representation of the factorization of the following quadratic polynomials:

1. $x^2 + 5x + 6$
2. $x^2 - 5x + 6$

MATERIAL REQUIRED
Glazed papers (blue, green, orange, yellow, and pink), white sheet of paper, geometry box, ruler, pair of scissors, and glue sticks.

THEORY
1. Knowledge of quadratic equations.
2. Splitting of the middle term of a quadratic polynomial as $ax^2 + bx + c = a(x + p)(x - q)$
   where $-p + q = -\dfrac{b}{a}, -pq = \dfrac{c}{a}$
3. Area of a rectangle $= l \times b$
4. Area of a square $= (\text{side})^2$

PROCEDURE
1. Every x^2 represents the area of pink-square of side x-units.
   Therefore, to represent $2x^2$, use two pink squares of side x units each. Take x as 3 units.

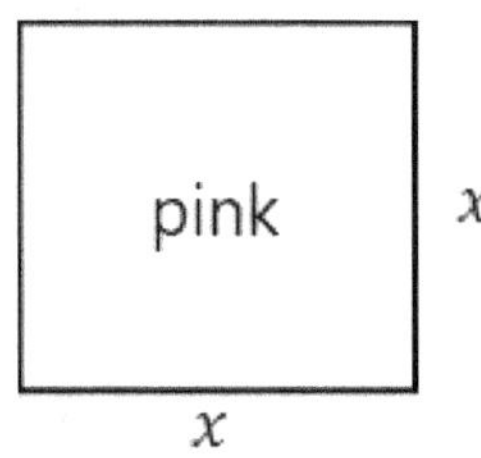

2. Every x represents the area of a green rectangular strip of dimensions $(1 \times x)$. [For $5x$, use 5 green strips each of dimensions $(1 \times x)$]

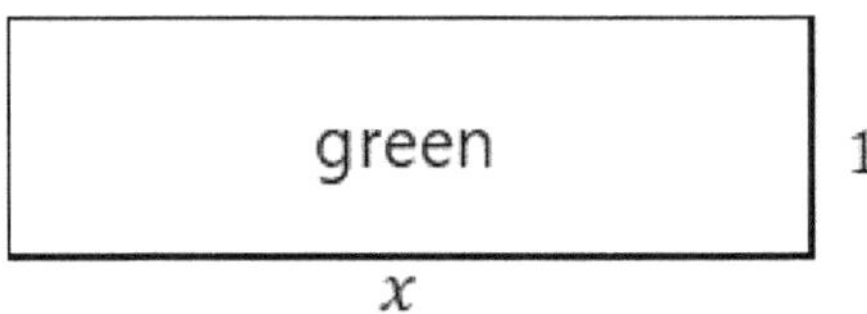

3. Every $(-x)$ is represented by a blue rectangular strip of dimensions $(1 \times x)$.
   For $(-5x)$, use 5 blue strips each of dimensions $(1 \times x)$.

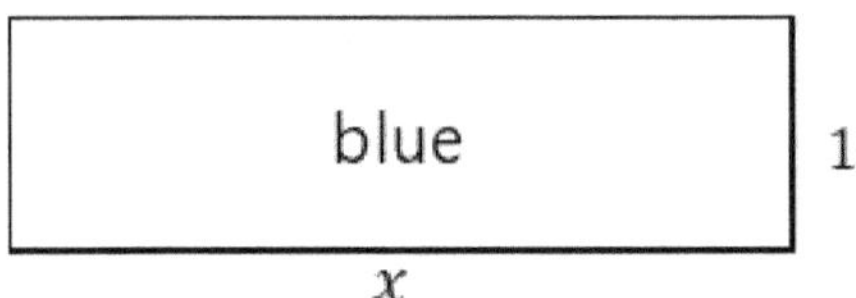

4. All positive integers are represented by yellow unit squares and all negative integers are shown by orange squares.

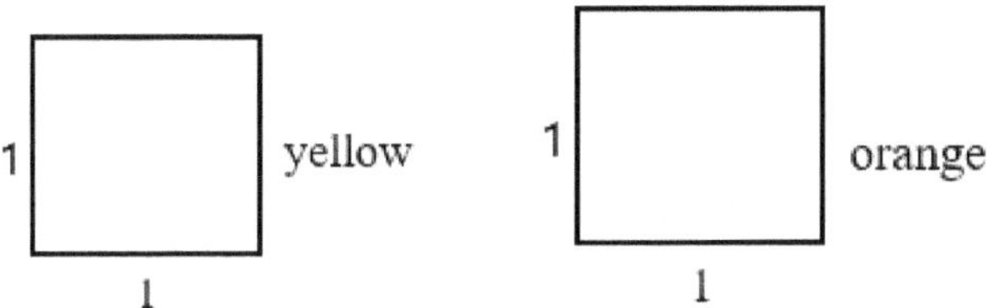

CASE I

Let us consider the expression $x^2 + 5x + 6$ which is of the form $(ax^2 + bx + c)$.

1. The polynomial $x^2 + 5x + 6 \Rightarrow x^2 + 3x + 2x + 6$ can be factorized as $(x + 3)(x + 2)$.
2. To present x^2, draw a pink square of x units [fig.(i)].

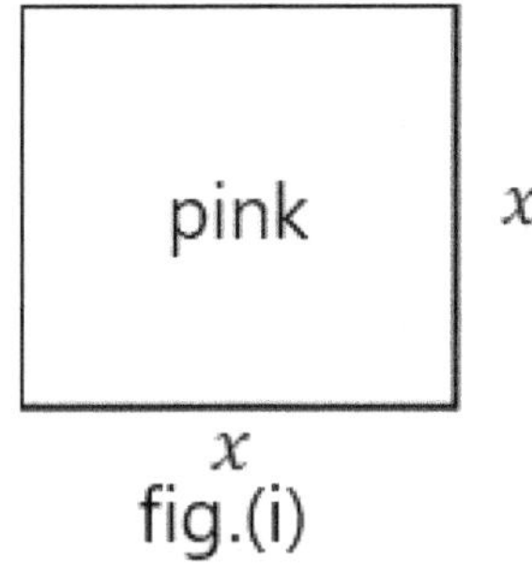

fig.(i)

3. To represent $3x$, draw three rectangular strips of green colour of dimension $(1 \times x)$ [fig. (ii)].

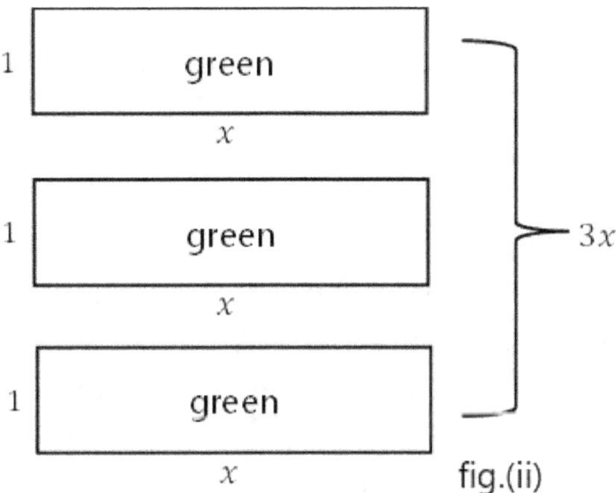

fig.(ii)

4. To represent $2x$, draw two green rectangular strips of dimensions $(1 \times x)$ [fig.(iii)].

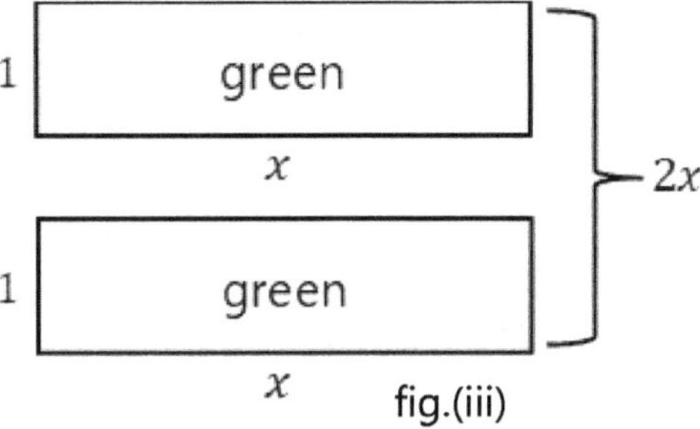

fig.(iii)

5. To represent 6, draw 6 yellow unit squares [fig. (iv)].

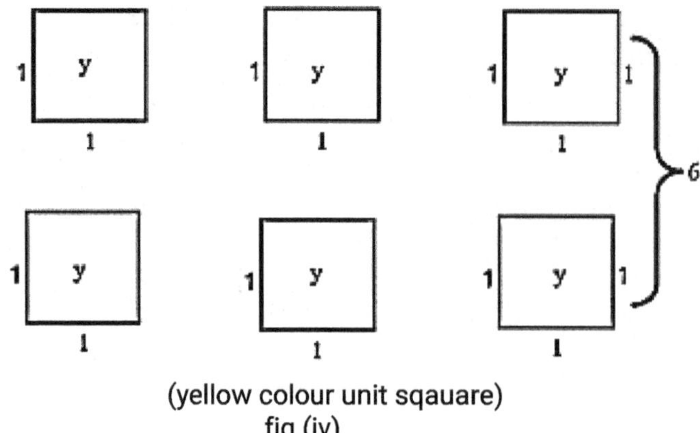

(yellow colour unit sqauare)
fig.(iv)

6. Cut all the strips from the glazed paper.
7. Now, paste all the strips together on the white sheet of paper as shown in fig.(v).

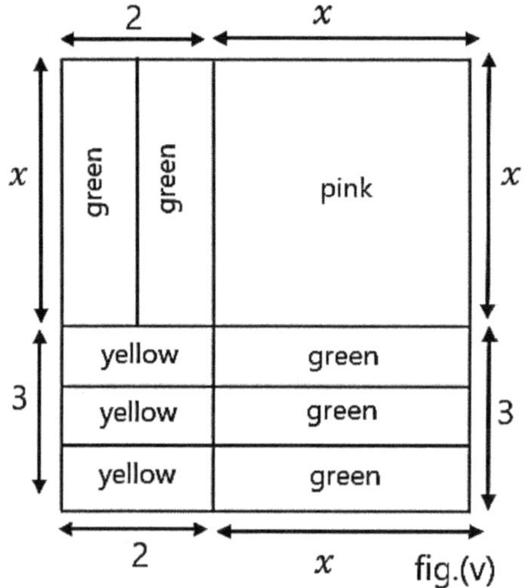

CASE II

Consider the expression $x^2 - 5x + 6$ and factorize it $x^2 - 3x - 2x + 6 = (x - 3)(x - 2)$.

1. Cut a pink square of dimension x units (say 8 units).
2. To represent 6, cut six yellow squares of dimension 1 unit.
3. To represent $-5x\{(-3x) + (-2x)\}$, cut five blue strips of dimension $(1 \times x)$.
4. Paste the pink square strips and all the yellow squares on a white sheet of paper as shown in fig. (vi).

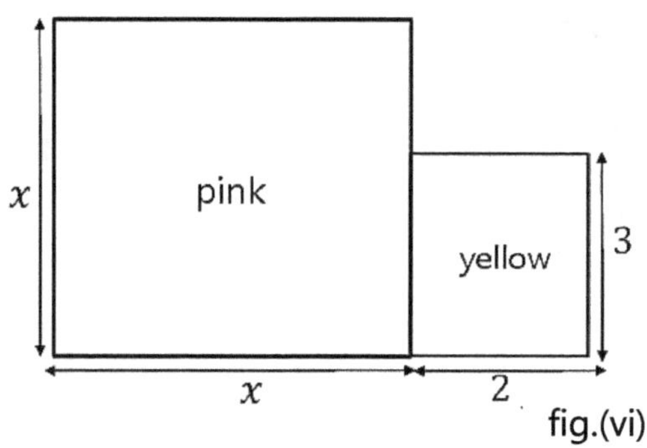

5. Now, paste all the five blue strips over the pink polygon as shown in fig.(vii).

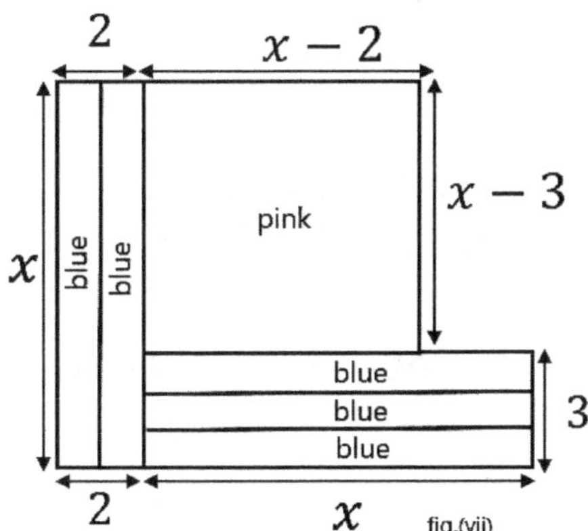

OBSERVATION AND CALCULATION

CASE I

$x^2 + 5x + 6$

Area of 5 green strips	$= 5x = 2x + 3x$
Area of pink square	$= x^2$
Area of 6 yellow unit squares	$= 6$
Total area of rectangle obtained	$= x^2 + 3x + 2x + 6$
	$= x^2 + 5x + 6$
	$= (x + 3)(x + 2)$

CASE II

$x^2 - 5x + 6$

Area of 5 blue rectangular strips	$= 5x$ (negative)
area of a pink square	$= x^2$
Area of 6 yellow unit squares	$= 6$
Total area of pink rectangle obtained after pasting all strips	$= (x - 2)(x - 3)$
	$= x^2 - 2x - 3x + 6$
	$= x^2 - 5x + 6x$

$$\therefore \quad x^2 - 5x + 6 = (x - 3)(x - 2)$$

RESULT

We verified the factors of two quadratic polynomials geometrically by papercutting and pasting.

LEARNING OUTCOME

Above method gives us the geometrical interpretation of the factorization of quadratic expressions of the form $ax^2 + bx + c$ or $ax^2 - bx + c$.

REMARKS

1. Pasting blue strips over a pink area means reducing pink area.
2. The pink portion so obtained represents the factors of the given quadratic expression.
3. Students may take different colour combinations.

By using paper cutting and pasting method, represent the factors of the following quadratic expressions:

1. $x^2 - x - 6$
2. $2x^2 + 5x + 2$

VIVA-VOCE

Question 1. How many linear factors can be in a quadratic polynomial?

Answer: 2 linear factors.

Question 2. Find two numbers whose sum is 1 and the product is -12.

Answer: -3 and 4

Question 3. Factorize: $x^2 + 7x + 12$.

Answer: $(x + 3)(x + 4)$

Question 4. Find two numbers whose sum is 0 and the product is -6.

Answer: $\sqrt{6}$ and $-\sqrt{6}$

Question 5. Is $y^2 + \dfrac{2}{y} + 5$ a polynomial?

Answer: No, as a power of y in $\dfrac{2}{y}$ is -1.

Question 6. Give one example of a binomial.

Answer: $(x + 5y)$.

Question 7. Is $2 + x^2 + x$ a polynomial?

Answer: Yes.

Question 8. What is the degree of $ax^2 + bx + c$?

Answer: 2.

Question 9. Write the product of $(2x - 1)(x + 1)$.

Answer: $2x^2 + x - 1$

Question 10. What is the degree of a quadratic polynomial?

Answer: The degree of a quadratic polynomial is 2.

MULTIPLE CHOICE QUESTION

Question 1.
The expression $x^2 - 21x + 20$ is factorized as
(a) $(x + 20)(x - 1)$
(b) $(x + 20)(x + 1)$
(c) $(x - 20)(x - 1)$
(d) $(x - 20)(x + 1)$

Question 2.
$x^2 - 5x + 6$ is factorized as
(a) $(x - 2)(x - 3)$
(b) $(x + 2)(x + 3)$
(c) $(x - 2)(x + 3)$
(d) $(x + 2)(x - 3)$

Question 3.
One of the factors of $x^2 - 3x + 2$ is
(a) $x + 2$
(b) $x + 1$
(c) $x - 1$
(d) $x + 3$

Question 4.
The factorization of $3x^2 - 14x - 5$ by splitting the middle term is
(a) $(x - 5)(3x + 1)$
(b) $(x + 5)(3x + 1)$
(c) $(x - 5)(3x - 1)$
(d) $(x + 5)(3x - 1)$

Question 5.
If one zero of the quadratic polynomials $x^2 + 3x + k$ is 2, then the value of k is
(a) 10
(b) −10
(c) 5
(d) −5

Question 6.
$x^2 - 6x + 8$ is factorized as
(a) $(x + 4)(x - 2)$
(b) $(x - 4)(x - 2)$
(c) $(x - 4)(x + 2)$
(d) $(x + 4)(x + 2)$

Question 7.
$(x - 2)$ is a factor of
(a) $x^2 - 7x - 18$
(b) $x^2 - 7x + 18$
(c) $x^2 + 7x + 18$
(d) $x^2 + 7x - 18$

Question 8.
$(x^2 - 4x)(x^2 - 4x - 1) - 20$ is factorized as
(a) $(x + 5)(x + 1)(x + 2)^2$
(b) $(x - 5)(x - 1)(x - 2)^2$
(c) $(x + 5)(x + 1)(x - 2)^2$
(d) $(x - 5)(x + 1)(x - 2)^2$

Question 9.
The factorization of $84 - 2x - 2x^2$ is
(a) $(x + 7)(12 - x)$
(b) $(x - 6)(14 + x)$
(c) $2(6 + x)(7 - x)$
(d) $2(6 - x)(7 + x)$

Question 10.
Zeroes of the polynomial $x^2 + 4x - 5$ are
(a) −1, 1
(b) 1, −5
(c) 0, −5
(d) −1, 5

ANSWER KEY

1.(a)	2.(a)	3.(c)	4.(d)	5.(b)	6.(b)	7.(d)	8.(d)	9.(d)	10.(b)

ACTIVITY 6

OBJECTIVE
To verify the identity $a^2 - b^2 = (a + b)(a - b)$ by paper cutting and pasting.

MATERIAL REQUIRED
White sheets of paper, two glazed papers (pink and blue), a pair of scissors, a geometry box, and gluestick.

THEORY
1. Area of square $= a^2$, where the side of a square$=$ a.
2. Area of rectangle $= l \times b$.

PROCEDURE
Take any two distinct values of a and b $(a > b)$ say $a = 5$ units, $b = 3$ units.
1. Draw a pink square of side 5 units and name it as ABCD as shown in fig.(i).

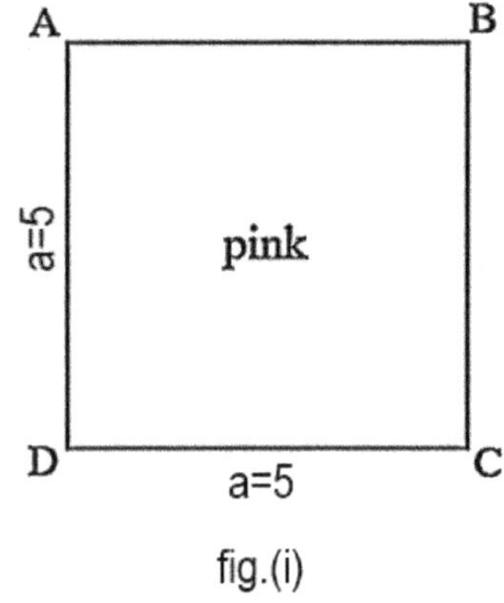

fig.(i)

2. Draw a blue square of side 3 units and name it as EFGH as shown in fig.(ii).

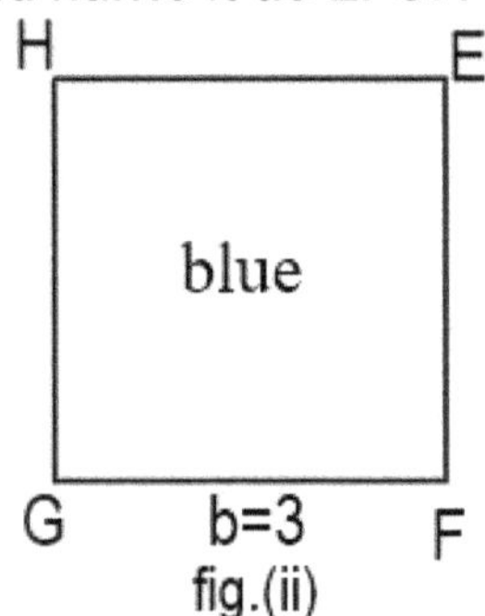

fig.(ii)

3. Cut these squares from glazed papers.
4. Paste two squares on a white sheet of paper. Square EFGH is pasted over square ABCD as shown in fig. (iii).

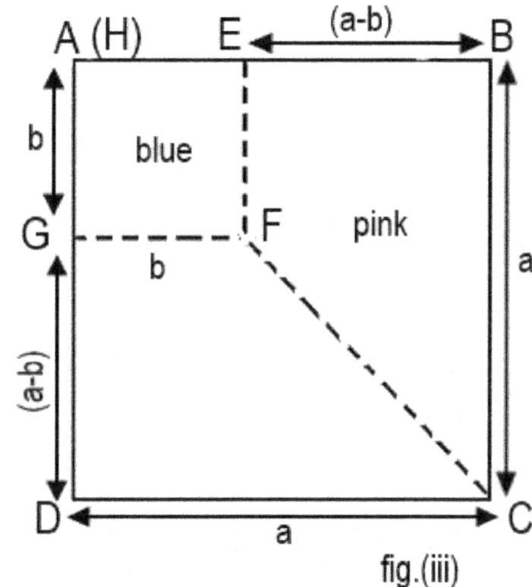

5. Join FC. Cut the pink portion along with FC and dotted lines. We get two quadrilaterals as EFCB and GFCD.
6. Now, place these two quadrilaterals on other white sheets of paper such that we get a rectangle. One piece of the quadrilateral is reversed to the other as shown in fig.(iv) and fig.(v).

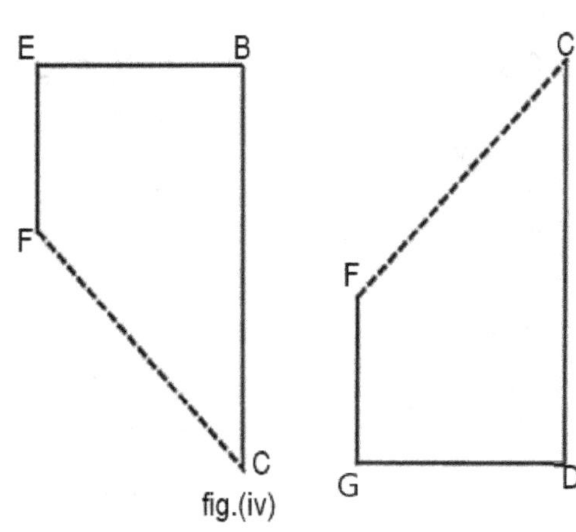

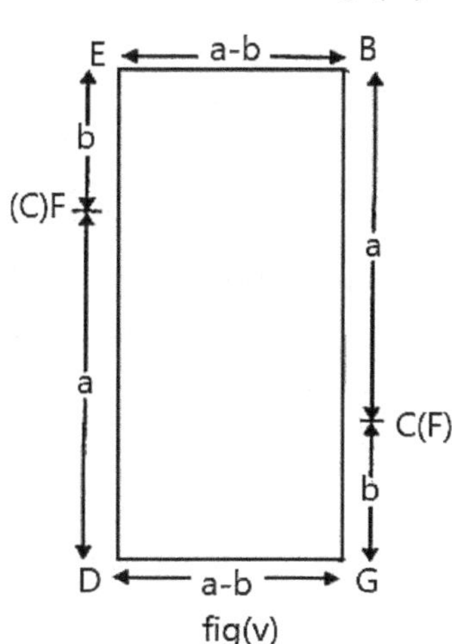

OBSERVATION AND CALCULATION

In fig. (i),
Area of square ABCD $= a^2 = (5)^2 = 25$ sq. units.
fig. (ii),
Area of square EFGH $= b^2 = (3)^2 = 9$ sq. units
fig. (iii),

$$= \text{Area of quadrilateral EBCF } + \text{ Area of quadrilateral GFCD}$$
$$= \text{Area of ABCD } - \text{ Area of square EFGH}$$
$$= (a^2 - b^2) \text{ sq. units}$$
$$= 25 - 9$$
$$= 16 \text{ sq. units...} \quad (i)$$

fig. (v), Area of rectangle EDGB $= \text{EB} \times \text{ED}$
$$= (a - b)(a + b)$$
$$= (5 - 3)(5 + 3)$$
$$= 2 \times 8$$
$$= 16 \text{ sq. units ... (ii)}$$

From (i) and (ii), we have
$$a^2 - b^2 = (a - b)(a + b)$$

RESULT
The identity $(a^2 - b^2) = (a + b)(a - b)$ is verified by paper cutting and pasting.

LEARNING OUTCOME
The identity $(a^2 - b^2) = (a + b)(a - b)$ is verified geometrically and can be verified by taking any other values of a and b.

ACTIVITY TIME
Verify $(a^2 - b^2) = (a + b)(a - b)$ by two different coloured papers, by taking different values of a and b.

e.g., $a = 7, b = 3$

VIVA-VOCE

Question 1. Which algebraic identity should be used to evaluate $64^2 - 36^2$?
Answer: $a^2 - b^2 = (a + b)(a - b)$

Question 2. Is the identity $a^2 - b^2 = (a + b)(a - b)$, holds for all real values of a and b ?
Answer: Yes

Question 3. Is $x^2 - y^2$ a monomial?
Answer: No, $x^2 - y^2$ is a binomial because it has two terms.

Question 4. Find the degree of an identity $a^2 - b^2 = (a - b)(a + b)$.
Answer: The degree of identity is two.

Question 5. Write the places where the algebraic identity $a^2 - b^2 = (a - b)(a + b)$ is used.
Answer: This identity is used in solving the quadratic equation, mensuration problem, factorization of polynomial, etc.

Question 6. If we take both negative variables, then there is no effect of algebraic identity.
Answer: No,
We know $a^2 - b^2 = (a + b)(a - b)$
Suppose we take
$a = -a$ and $b = -b$,
then
$(-a)^2 - (-b)^2 = (-a - b)(-a + b)$
$\Rightarrow a^2 - b^2 = (a - b)(a + b)$

Question 7. Is the algebraic identity $a^2 - b^2 = (a + b)(a - b)$ is also true if any one of the variables in the given identity is zero?
Answer: Yes, suppose $b = 0$, then
$a^2 - 0^2 = (a + 0)(a - 0)$
$\Rightarrow a^2 = a^2$, true.

Question 8. If the sides of a rectangle are $(\sqrt{3} + \sqrt{2})$ units and $(\sqrt{3} - \sqrt{2})$ units, then what will be its area?
Answer: 1 sq unit.

MULTIPLE CHOICE QUESTION

Question 1.
Which of the following is the numerical coefficient of x^2y^2 ?
(a) 0
(b) 1
(c) x^2
(d) y^2

Question 2.
Which of the following is the numerical coefficient of $-5xy$?
(a) 5
(b) $-x$
(c) -5
(d) $-y$

Question 3.
pqr is what type of polynomial?
(a) Monomial
(b) Binomial
(c) Trinomial
(d) None of these

Question 4.
The value of $x^2 - 5$ at $x = -1$ is-
(a) -2
(b) -1
(c) -4
(d) -5

Question 5.
Which of the following is obtained by subtracting $x^2 - y^2$ from $y^2 - x^2$?
(a) $-2(x^2 - y^2)$
(b) $-2(x^2 + y^2)$
(c) $2(x^2 + y^2)$
(d) $2(x^2 - y^2)$

Question 6.
Which of the following is the value of $\left(\frac{x+1}{x}\right)^2$?
(a) $\frac{x^2+1}{x^2}$
(b) $\frac{x^2-1}{x^2+2}$
(c) $\frac{x^2+1}{x^2+2}$
(d) $\frac{x^2+1}{x^2+2x}$

Question 7.
$a^2 - b^2$ is a product of
(a) $(a + b)(a - b)$
(b) $(a + b)(a + b)$
(c) $(a - b)(a - b)$
(d) None of these

Question.8.
What degree does $x^3 - x^2y^2 - 8y^2 + 2$ have?
(a) 2
(b) 3
(c) 4
(d) 7

Question.9.
What is the value of $5x^{25} - 3x^{32} + 2x^{-12}$ at $x = 1$?
(a) 0
(b) 2
(c) 4
(d) None of these

Question.10.
What is the product of $(x + a)$ and $(x + b)$?
(a) $x^2 + (a - b)x + ab$
(b) $x^2 + (a + b)x - ab$
(c) $x^2 + (a + b)x - ab$
(d) $x^2 + (a + b)x + ab$

ANSWER KEY

1.(b)	2.(c)	3.(a)	4.(c)	5.(a)	6.(c)	7.(a)	8.(b)	9.(c)	10.(d)

ACTIVITY (7)

OBJECTIVE

To verify the identity $a^3 + b^3 = (a + b)(a^2 - ab + b^2)$ geometrically by using sets of unit cubes.

MATERIAL REQUIRED

A set of 56 cubes each has dimensions $(1 \times 1 \times 1)$ cubic unit. Cubes may be of wood, plastic, cardboard, or thermocol.

THEORY

1. Volume of cube $= (\text{edge})^3$
2. Volume of cuboid $= (l \times b \times h)$

PROCEDURE

To verify the identity $a^3 + b^3$, we shall take $a = 3$ unit. and $b = 1$ unit.

1. Arrange 28 cubes such that we get a cube of $3 \times 3 \times 3$ cubic units and a single unit cube of $b = 1$ unit. as shown in fig. (i) and fig.(ii).

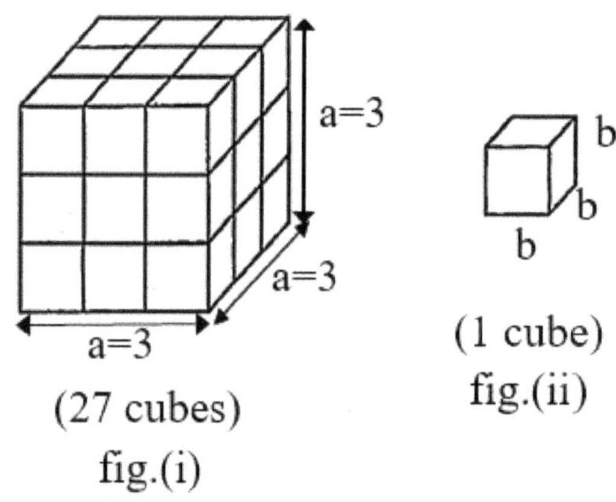

2. Now we will use second set of 28 cubes. Consider one stack (24 cubes) as $\{a \times (a + b) \times (a - b)\}$ cubic units i.e., $(3 \times 4 \times 2)$ cubic units and arrange as shown in fig. (iii):

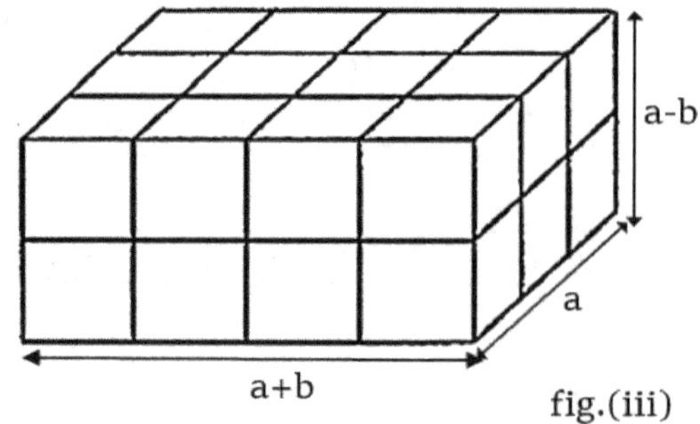

3. Consider another stack of 4 cubes such as $(a + b)(b)(b)$ i.e., $(4)(1)(1)$ cubic units. Arrange them as shown in fig. (iv).

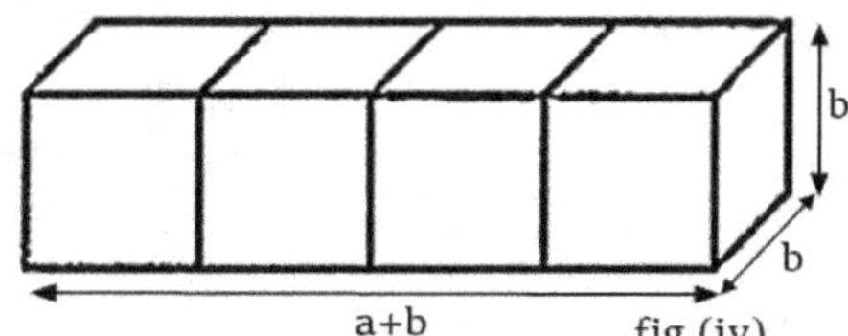

OBSERVATION AND CALCULATION

As the arrangements are shown in [fig. (i), fig. (ii)] and [fig. (iii), fig. (iv)], have an equal number of cubes, therefore, the total volume in both cases must be same.

In fig(i) and fig.(ii)

Volume of cube in fig. (i) $=$ volume of 27-unit cubes $= a^3$

Volume of cube of 1 unit $= b^3$

Total volume of 28 cubes $= a^3 + b^3$

In fig. (iii) and (iv),

Volume of cuboid of 24-unit cubes $= (a + b)(a - b)(a)$

Volume of cuboid of 4 unit cubes $= (a + b)b^2$

$$\text{Total volume of 28 cubes} = (a + b)(a - b)(a) + (a + b)(b^2)$$
$$= (a + b)(a^2 - ab + b^2)$$

From (i) and (ii), we have

$$\therefore a^3 + b^3 = (a + b)(a^2 - ab + b^2)$$

RESULT

The identity $\therefore a^3 + b^3 = (a + b)(a^2 - ab + b^2)$ is verified geometrically by using cubes and cuboids.

LEARNING OUTCOME

Algebraic identity $\therefore a^3 + b^3 = (a + b)(a^2 - ab + b^2)$ is verified geometrically. This activity can be performed by using different colours of cubes as shown in fig. (i), (ii), (iii) and (iv). We have learnt making of cuboids of various dimensions by using unit cubes and adding and subtracting cuboids.

ACTIVITY TIME

By using different values of a and b, students can verify the identity $a^3 + b^3$, e.g., $a = 6, b = 2$ and also find volume of different cubes and cuboids used for this activity.

VIVA-VOCE

Question 1. What is the expanded form of $a^3 - b^3$?

Answer: The expanded form of $a^3 - b^3 = (a - b)(a^2 + ab + b^2)$

Question 2. If $(a^2 + ab + b^2) = 0$, then what will be the value of $a^3 - b^3$?

Answer: $\because a^3 - b^3 = (a - b)(a^2 + ab + b^2)$
$\therefore a^3 - b^3 = 0 \quad [\because a^2 + ab + b^2 = 0]$

Question 3. If $x = y$, then what will be the value of $x^3 - y^3$?

Answer: Now, $x^3 - y^3 = x^3 - x^3$
$= 0 \, [\because x = y]$

Question 4. What is the degree of the expression $y^3 - x^3$?

Answer: The degree of the given expression is 3.

Question 5. Write the real zero of $z^3 + 1$.

Answer: -1

Question 6. The product of $(x)^2, -(x)^3,$ $-(x)^4$ is? **Answer:** x^9	**Question 7.** The number of like terms in $9x^3,$ $16x^2y, -8x^3, 12xy, 6x^3$ is? **Answer:** 3

MULTIPLE CHOICE QUESTION

Question 1

The factorization of $p^3 + 0.008$ is:
(a) $(p + 0.2)(p^2 + 0.2p + 0.004)$
(b) $(p - 0.2)(p^2 - 0.2p + 0.004)$
(c) $(p + 0.2)(p^2 - 0.2p + 0.004)$
(d) $(p - 0.2)(p^2 + 0.2p + 0.004)$

Question 2

$(51)^3 =$
(a) 136251
(b) 136521
(c) 132651
(d) 135621

Question 3

If $2x + 3y = 13$ and $xy = 4$, the value of $8x^3 + 27y^3$ is:
(a) 3133
(b) 3331
(c) 1216
(d) 1261

Question 4

The simplification of $(y + 1)^3 + (y - 1)^3$ is
(a) $2y^3 - 6y$
(b) $2y^3 + 6y$
(c) $y^3 + 6y$
(d) $y^3 - 6y$

Question 5

If $\frac{x}{y} + \frac{y}{x} = 1 (x, y \neq 0)$, then the value of $x^3 + y^3$
(a) 0
(b) 1
(c) 2
(d) -1

Question 6

If $x + \frac{1}{x} = 2$, then $x^3 + \frac{1}{x^3} =$
(a) 64
(b) 14
(c) 8
(d) 2

Question 7.

If $\left(x + \frac{1}{x}\right) = 3$, then $\left(x^6 + \frac{1}{x^6}\right)$ is:
(a) 927
(b) 414
(c) 364
(d) 322

Question 8.

If $\left(x^3 + \frac{1}{x^3}\right) = 110$, then $\left(x + \frac{1}{x}\right) =$
(a) 5
(b) 10
(c) 15
(d) None of these

Question 9.

Check weather $x = 4$ is the zero of $(64a^3 + 1)$:
(a) No
(b) Yes
(c) Can't say
(d) None of these

Question 10.

Write the degree of $(3 + a)(9 + a^2 - 3a)$:
(a) 1
(b) 3
(c) 2
(d) None of these

ANSWER KEY

1. (a)	2. (c)	3. (d)	4. (b)	5. (a)	6. (d)	7. (d)	8. (a)	9. (a)	10. (c)

ALGEBRAIC IDENTITY
$(a + b)^3 = a^3 + b^3 + 3a^2b + 3ab^2$

OBJECTIVE
To verify the identity $(a + b)^3 = a^3 + b^3 + 3a^2b + 3ab^2$ geometrically by using sets of unit cubes.

MATERIAL REQUIRED
A set of 128 plastic cubes or wooden cubes with dimensions (1unit x 1unit x1unit).

THEORY
1. Volume of a cube $= (\text{edge})^3$
2. Volume of a cuboid $= l \times b \times h$

PROCEDURE
To verify the identity $(a + b)^3 = a^3 + b^3 + 3a^2b + 3ab^2$, we shall take value of a = 3 units and value of b = 1unit.

1. First, we will make a cube of dimensions $(a + b)$ i.e., $(3 + 1 = 4$ units). For this, we will use 64-unit cubes and arrange them as shown in fig.(i).

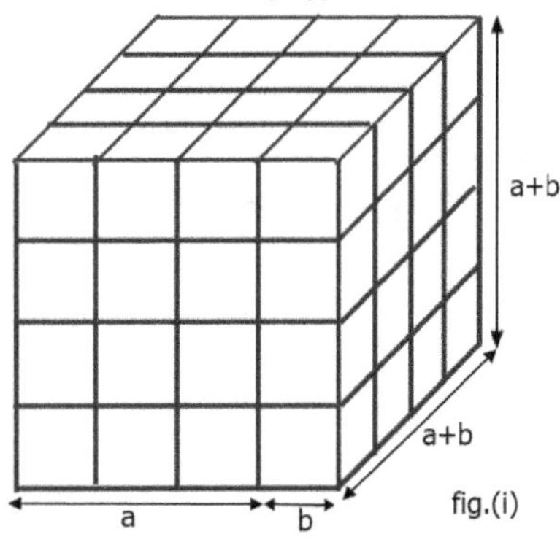

2. From other sets of 64 cubes, we will make arrangements as shown in figures.

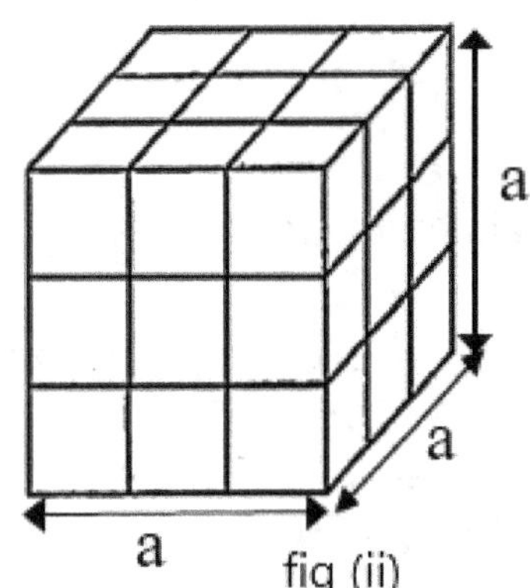

3. Arrange 27 cubes such that $a \times a \times a$ cube is formed i.e., $3 \times 3 \times 3$ set is formed in fig.(ii).
4. Arrange 9 cubes such that 3 columns of 3 cubes are formed as shown in fig. (iii). Make 3 sets of such arrangements.

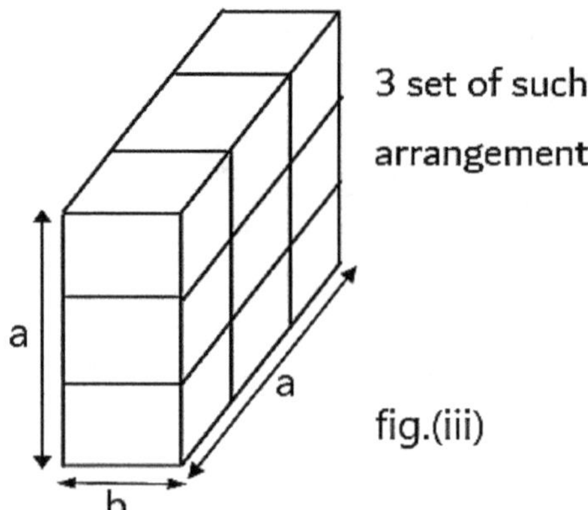

4. Arrange 3 cubes such that 1 column of 3 cubes is formed as shown in fig. (iv). Make 3 sets of such arrangements.

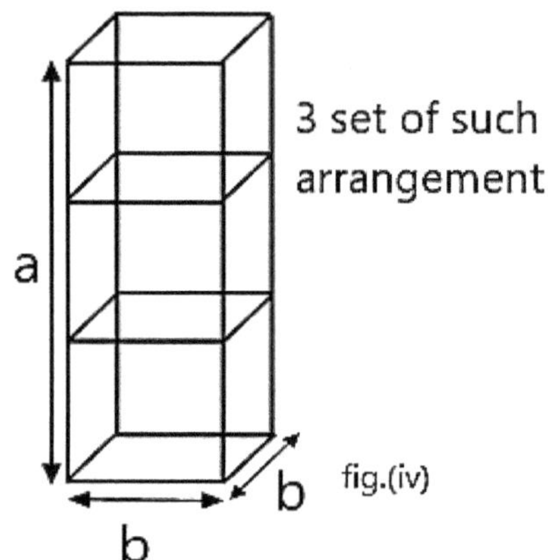

5. Last arrangement consists of only 1 cube of volume b^3 [fig (v)].

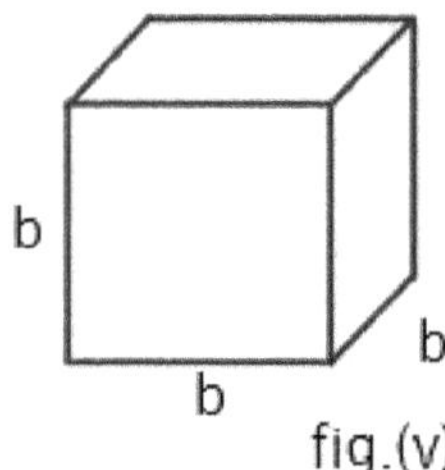

OBSERVATION AND CALCULATION

In fig. (i) we have used 64 cubes i.e., $(a+b)^3$

Other set of 64 cubes are arranged in following manner:

1. Volume of cube in fig. (ii) $= a^3$
2. Volume of cuboids in fig.(iii) $= 3(a)(a)(b) = 3ba^2$
3. Volume of cuboids in fig. (iv) $= 3(a)(b)(b) = 3ab^2$
4. Volume of cube in fig. (v) $= b^3$

Total volume of cube in fig. (i) = Total volume of cubes and cuboids in fig. (ii),(iii), (iv), and (v)

$$(a+b)^3 = a^3 + b^3 + 3a^2b + 3ab^2$$

Hence, this identity is verified geometrically.

RESULT

The identity $(a + b)^3 = a^3 + b^3 + 3a^2b + 3ab^2$ is verified geometrically by using cubes and cuboids.

LEARNING OUTCOME

In this way, students can learn the concept of verifying the identity geometrically by adding the volume of cubes and cuboids.

ACTIVITY TIME

Students must perform this activity for any other values of a and b, e.g., $a = 4, b = 1$ and find volumes of different cubes and cuboids used in this activity.

VIVA-VOCE

Question 1. Expand $(a + b)^3$.
Answer: $(a + b)^3 = a^3 + b^3 + 3ab(a + b)$.

Question 2. If $x + y = 6$ and $xy = 7$, then $x^3 - y^3 =$?
Answer: 90.

Question 3. If $x + y = 4$ and $xy = 5$, then $x^3 + y^3 =$?
Answer: 4.

Question 4. What is the value of $(a + b)^3$, if $a + b = 0$?
Answer: 0.

Question 5. The value of $x^3 + y^3$ when $x = 1, y = 2$ is?
Answer: 9.

Question 6. How many terms are there in the expression $5xy^2$?
Answer: 1.

Question 7. The factors of $a^2 - 1 - 2x - x^2$ is?
Answer: $(a + 1 + x)(a - 1 - x)$.

Question 8. The degree of the polynomial $5x^3 - 6x^3y + 4y^2 - 8$ is:
Answer. 3.

MULTIPLE CHOICE QUESTION

Question 1.
Expansion of $(x + y)^3$ is
(a) $x^3 + y^3 + 3x^2y - 3xy^2$
(b) $x^3 - y^3 + 3x^2y + 3xy^2$
(c) $x^3 + y^3 - 3x^2y + 3xy^2$
(d) $x^3 + y^3 + 3x^2y + 3xy^2$

Question 2.
The coefficient of x^2 in the expansion of $(x + 3)^3$
(a) 1
(b) 2
(c) 3
(d) −1

Question 3.
By using identity 4, the value of $(25)^3 + (10)^3$ is
(a) 17125
(b) 27125
(c) 16625
(d) 14625

Question 4.
If $a^3 + b^3 = 200$, $a + b = 5$, find the value of (ab)?
(a) 16
(b) 10
(c) 5
(d) None of these

Question 5.
Value of $(1002)^3$ is
(a) 1060012008
(b) 106012006
(c) 1006012008
(d) None of these

Question 6.
Value of $(103)^3$ is
(a) 1092717
(b) 1092727
(c) 109272
(d) None of these

Question 7.
Value of $23^3 - 17^3$ is
(a) 2754
(b) 5724
(c) 2745
(d) 7254

Question 8.
Expansion of $(2 + z)^3$ is
(a) $8 + z^3 + 12z + 6z^2$
(b) $8 + z^3 - 12z + 6z^2$
(c) $8 - z^3 - 12z - 6z^2$
(d) $8 - z^3 + 12z + 6z^2$

Question 9.
Evaluate, $(50)^3$ using identity $(a + b)^3$:
(a) 125000
(b) 125999
(c) 135000
(d) None of these

Question 10.
The value of $(2x + 3y)^3$ is
(a) $8x^3 + 27y^3 + 36x^2y + 54xy^2$
(b) $8x^3 - 27y^3 + 36x^2y + 54xy^2$
(c) $8x^3 - 27y^3 - 36x^2y - 54xy^2$
(d) None of these

ANSWER KEY

| 1. (d) | 2. (a) | 3. (c) | 4. (c) | 5. (c) | 6. (b) | 7. (d) | 8. (a) | 9. (a) | 10. (a) |

ALGEBRAIC IDENTITY
$$(a^3 - b^3) = (a - b)(a^2 + ab + b^2)$$

OBJECTIVE
To verify the identity $a^3 - b^3 = (a-b)(a^2 + ab + b^2)$ geometrically by using sets of unit cubes.

MATERIAL REQUIRED
A set of 53 plastic or wooden cubes each of dimensions ($1\ unit \times 1\ unit \times 1\ unit$)

THEORY
Volume of a cube = (Edge)^3
Volume of a cuboid = $l \times$ b $\times$ h
$a^3 - b^3 = (a-b)(a^2 + ab + b^2)$

PROCEDURE
To verify $a^3 - b^3 = (a-b)(a^2 + ab + b^2)$ Let $a = 3$ and $b = 1$.
1. Take 27 cubes and place them to form a stack consisting of 9 columns, each column con-sisting of 3 cubes [fig. (i)].
2. Remove one cube from this stack get a stack of 26 cubes (Arrangement I)

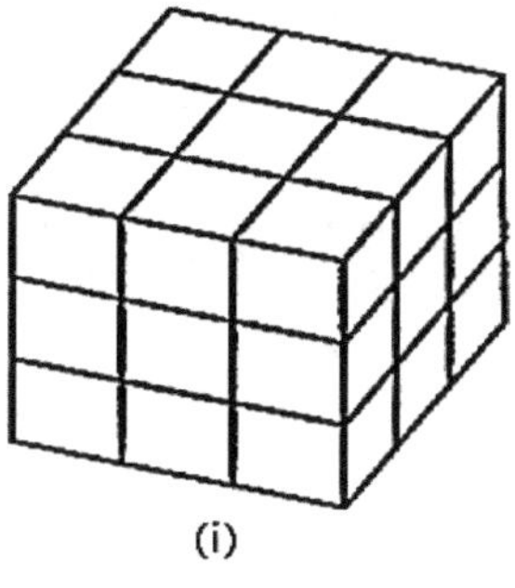

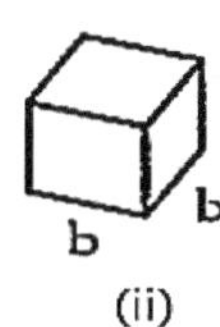

Arrangement-I

fig.(i)

3. Make arrangement II of 26 cubes. This arrangement consists of three stacks.
    (a) The first stack consists of 18 cubes such as 9 columns of two cubes each.
    (b) The second stack consists of 6 cubes such as two rows of three cubes each.
    (c) The third stack consists of 1 row of 2 cubes.

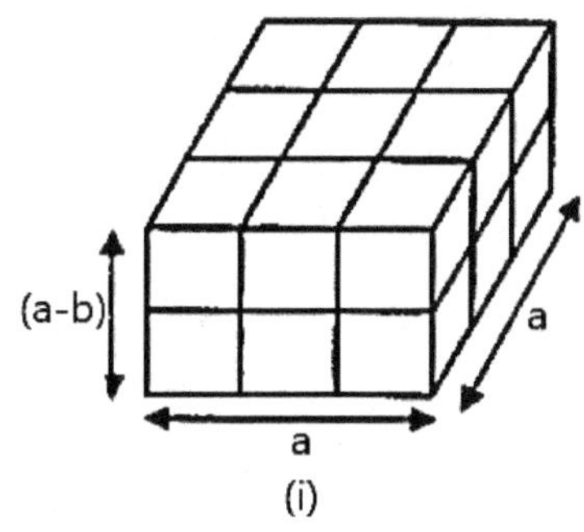

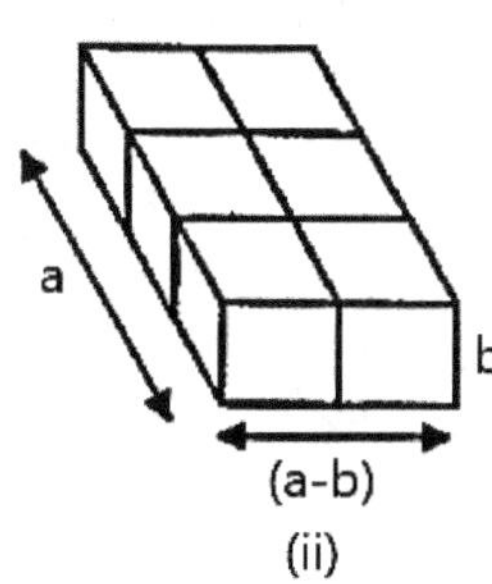

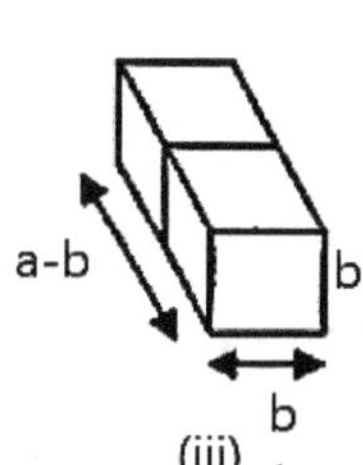

Arrangement-II

fig.(ii)

OBSERVATION

Since the two arrangements have equal number of cubes (each arrangement has 26 cubes), the total volume in both the arrangements must be equal.

1. Volume of arrangement I

    Volume of stack in fig. 1. (i) $= a^3$

    Volume of stack in fig. 1. (ii) $= b^3$

    $\therefore$ Volume of arrangement I $=$ Volume of stack in fig. 1(i) $-$ Volume of stack in fig. 1(ii)

    $$= a^3 - b^3$$

2. Volume of arrangement II

    Volume of stack in fig. 2 (i) $= (a - b)a^2$

    Volume of stack in fig. 2(ii) $= (a - b)ab$

    Volume of stack in fig. 2 (iii) $= (a - b)b^2$

    Volume of arrangement II $= (a - b)a^2 + (a - b)ab + (a - b)b^2$

    $$= (a - b)(a^2 + ab + b^2)$$

    Since the number of cubes in the arrangement I and II is equal.

    $$\therefore a^3 - b^3 = (a - b)(a^2 + ab + b^2)$$

RESULT

The identity $a^3 - b^3 = (a - b)(a^2 + ab + b^2)$ is verified geometrically by using cubes and cuboids.

LEARNING OUTCOME

In this way, students can learn the concept of verifying the identity geometrically by adding different cubes and cuboids.

ACTIVITY TIME

Students can perform this activity for any other values of a and b e.g., $a = 6$, $b = 2$ and find volumes of different cubes and cuboids through this activity.

VIVA-VOCE

Question 1. Define a cube.

Answer: A cube having equal length, breadth and height is called a cube

Question 2. Define a cuboid.

Answer: A cuboid or parallelopiped is a solid having six rectangular faces and eight vertices.

Question 3. Factorize $a^3 - b^3$.

Answer: $a^3 - b^3 = (a - b)(a^2 + ab + b^2)$

Question 4. Find the volume of a cube whose side is 8 cm.

Answer: Volume of the cube $= (\text{ side })^3 = (8 \text{ cm})^3 = 512 \text{ cm}^3$

Question 5. What is the value of $4^3 - 3^3$?

Answer: $(4 - 3)(16 + 9 + 12) = 37$.

Question 6. What is the simplification of $8^3 - 2^3$

Answer: $(8 - 2)(64 + 4 + 16) = 504$.

Question 7. Factorize: $27x^3 - 8y^3$.

Answer: $(3x - 2y)(9x^2 + 4y^2 + 6xy)$.

Question 8. Find $10^3 - 5^3$.

Answer: $(10 - 5)(100 + 25 + 50) = 875$.

Question 9. Write the real zero of $125x^3 - 1$.

Answer: $\dfrac{1}{5}$.

MULTIPLE CHOICE QUESTION

Question 1.
If $p - q = 1$ and $pq = 6$, then the value of $p^3 - q^3$:
(a) 12
(b) 19
(c) 15
(d) 18

Question 2.
The value of $\dfrac{(2.3)^3 - 0.027}{(2.3)^2 + 0.69 + 0.09}$ is:
(a) 3.127
(b) 2
(c) 2.237
(d) 3

Question 3.
The factorization of $1 - 64x^3$ is
(a) $(1 - 4x)(1 + 4x + 16x^2)$
(b) $(1 - 4x)(1 - 4x + 16x^2)$
(c) $(1 + 4x)(1 - 4x + 16x^2)$
(d) None of the above

Question 4.
If $x - y = 14$ and $xy = 21$, then the value of $x^3 - y^3$ is:
(a) 2969
(b) 3626
(c) 2492
(d) 3204

Question 5.
$x^6 - y^6$ equals to:
(a) $(x + y)(x - y)(x^2 - xy + y^2)(x^2 - xy + y^2)$
(b) $(x + y)(x + y)(x^2 + xy + y^2)(x^2 - xy + y^2)$
(c) $(x - y)(x - y)(x^2 + xy + y^2)(x^2 - xy + y^2)$
(d) $(x + y)(x - y)(x^2 + xy + y^2)(x^2 - xy + y^2)$

Question 6.
If $a - b = 4$ and $ab = 45$, then the value of $a^3 - b^3$ is:
(a) 406
(b) 604
(c) 460
(d) 640

Question 7.
If $a - b = 6$ and $ab = 20$, then the value of $a^3 - b^3$ is:
(a) 576
(b) 756
(c) 657
(d) None of these

Question 8.
If $a - b = -8$ and $ab = -12$, then $a^3 - b^3 =$
(a) -244
(b) -240
(c) -224
(d) -260

Question 9.
Write the coefficient of x^3 in $(365x^3 - 16y)$:
(a) 16
(b) -16
(c) 365
(d) None of these

Question 10.
Write the degree of $a^2 - b^2$
(a) 3
(b) 2
(c) 6
(d) None of these

ANSWER KEY

1. (b)	2. (b)	3. (a)	4. (b)	5. (d)	6. (b)	7. (a)	8. (c)	9. (c)	10. (b)

COORDINATE GEOMETRY

OBJECTIVE

To obtain the mirror image of a given geometrical figure with respect to x-axis and y-axis.

MATERIAL REQUIRED

Graph paper, pencil (coloured), eraser, ruler, and mirror.

THEORY

1. Plotting the points on the graph paper.
2. Cartesian system.
3. The perpendicular distance between the mirror and the image of point P is equal to the perpendicular distance between point P and the mirror.

PROCEDURE

1. Draw any figure on the graph paper in the first quadrant (say, a figure of stairs).
2. For stairs, plot some points say, A(3,0), B(3,1), C(2,1), D(2,2), E(1,2), F(1,3),G(0,3) with coloured pencils.
3. join A, B, C, D, E, F, G as shown in fig. (i).
4. Consider y-axis as a mirror.
5. Fold the graph along the y-axis to get the images of points A, B, C, D, E,F, G in the second quadrant as A', B', C', D', E', F', G' respectively as shown in fig.(i).
6. Join A', B', C', D', E', F', G' we get the image of the stairs.
7. Note down the coordinates of the image so formed and record them in observation Table 1.
8. Repeat the procedure for the same stairs with respect to the x-axis i.e., to get the image of the stairs taking the x-axis as a mirror.
9. Now, we will get the image in the fourth quadrant.
10. Note down the coordinates of the image along the x-axis and record in Table 2.

MIRROR IMAGE W.R.T. y-AXIS

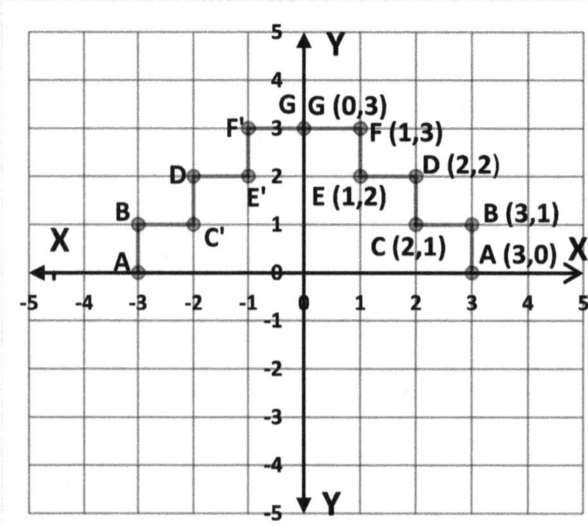

fig.(i)

MIRROR IMAGE W.R.T. x-AXIS

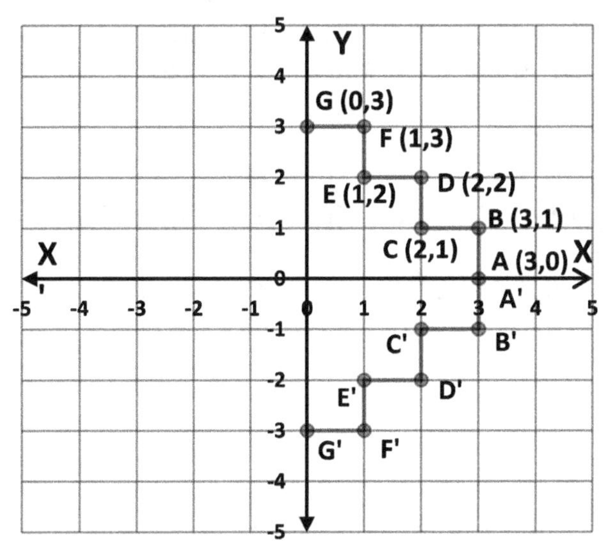

Mirror image
w.r.t. x-axis

fig.(ii)

OBSERVATION AND CALCULATION

Table 1 (Image along y-axis)

S. No.	Coordinates of Fig. ABCDEFG	Coordinates of image A′B′C′D′E′F′G′
1.	A(3,0)	A′(−3,0)
2.	B(3,1)	B′(−3,1)
3.	C(2,1)	C′(−2,1)
4.	D(2,2)	D′(−2,2)
5.	E(1,2)	E′(−1,2)
6.	F(1,3)	F′(−1,3)
7.	G(0,3)	G′(0,3)

Table 2 (Image along x-axis)

S. No.	Coordinates of Fig. ABCDEFG	Coordinates of image A' B' C' D' E' F' G'
1.	A(3,0)	A′(3,0)
2.	B(3,1)	B′(3,−1)
3.	C(2,1)	C′(2,−1)
4.	D(2,2)	D′(2,−2)
5.	E(1,2)	E′(1,−2)
6.	F(1,3)	F′(1,−3)
7.	G(0,3)	G′(0,−3)

RESULT
We have obtained the mirror images of figures along the x-axis and y-axis.

LEARNING OUTCOME
1. **Mirror image with respect to x-axis:** In this case, the image of P (x, y) becomes P $(x, -y)$.

Thus, to find the image of any point along the x-axis, we keep the x-coordinate same, and a sign of y-coordinate gets changed.Any point on the mirror remains the same.

2. **Mirror image with respect to y-axis:** In this case, the image of P (x, y) becomes P $(-x, y)$. Thus, to find the image of any point with respect to y-axis, we keep the y-coordinate same, and the sign of the x-coordinate gets changed.

ACTIVITY TIME

1. The same activity can be performed for other figures like quadrilaterals,triangles, stars, or any polygon.
2. Draw the mirror image of the figure shown, in the second quadrant by plotting different corner points of the figure.

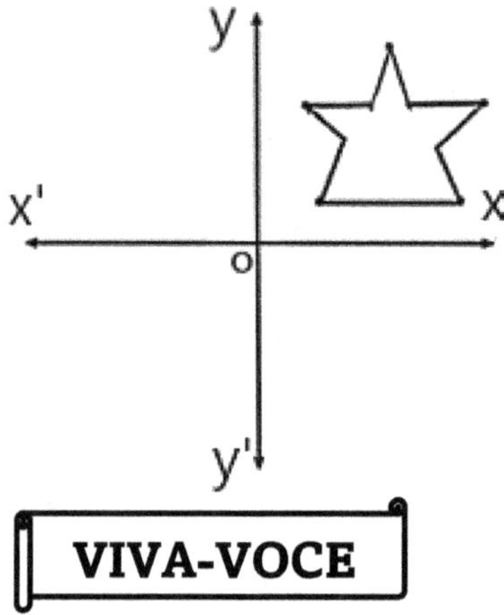

VIVA-VOCE

Question 1. What is the angle sum property of a quadrilateral?
Answer. The sum of all angles of a quadrilateral is a complete angle, i.e., 360°

Question 2. The sum of three angles of a quadrilateral is 280°. Find the measure of the fourth angle.
Answer. Fourth angle = 360° − 280° = 80°

Question 3. How many vertices a quadrilateral has?
Answer. A quadrilateral has 4 vertices.

Question 4. In which quadrilateral(s), diagonals are perpendicular to each other?
Answer. Rhombus.

Question 5. Is it true that the diagonals of a rhombus are equal?
Answer. No

Question 6. What are the conditions that any quadrilateral be a square?
Answer. (i) All four sides of a quadrilateral are equal.
(ii) Each angle of a quadrilateral is 90°.
(iii) Diagonals are equal and bisect each other.

Question 7. Is it true that a parallelogram is always a trapezium, but a trapezium is not always a parallelogram?
Answer. True

Question 8. Can all the angles of a quadrilateral be right angles? Give reason.
Answer. Yes, all the angles of a quadrilateral can be right angles. e.g., Square and rectangle.

Question 9. Is it true that every parallelogram is a rectangle?
Answer. No, only that parallelogram is rectangle whose all angles are 90°.

MULTIPLE CHOICE QUESTION

Question 1.
A point $P(x, y)$ lies in the 2nd quadrant. If the signs of x and y are interchanged then it lies in:
(a) 1st quadrant
(b) 2nd quadrant
(c) 3rd quadrant
(d) 4th quadrant

Question 2.
A point P(x, y) lies in the 4th quadrant. The signs of x and y are:
(a) $(-, +)$
(b) $(-, +)$
(c) $(+, -)$
(d) $(-, -)$

Question 3.
If $x > 0$ and $y < 0$, then the point (x, y) lies in:
(a) 1st quadrant
(b) 2nd quadrant
(c) 3rd quadrant
(d) 4th quadrant

Question 4.
Which of the following points do not lie on the line $y = 2x + 1$
(a) $(1, 3)$
(b) $(2, 5)$
(c) $(3, 7)$
(d) $(5, 12)$

Question 5.
If the coordinates of the two points are P$(-2, 3)$ and Q$(-3, 5)$, then (abscissa of P) - (abscissa of Q) is:
(a) -5
(b) 1
(c) -1
(d) -2

Question 6.
If y coordinate of a point is zero, then the point always lies:
(a) in first quadrant
(b) in second quadrant
(c) on x-axis
(d) on y-axis

Question 7.
The coordinates of a point having coordinate 4 and lying on y-axis are given by:
(a) $(4, 0)$
(b) $(0, 4)$
(c) $(1, 4)$
(d) $(4, 2)$

Question 8.
The perpendicular distance of the point P$(3, 4)$ from the y-axis is:
(a) 3 units
(b) 4 units
(c) 5 units
(d) 7 units

Question 9.
Write the abscissa and coordinate of $(-5, 6)$:
(a) abscissa $= 6$, ordinate $= -5$
(b) abscissa $= -5$, ordinate $= 6$
(c) abscissa $= 5$, ordinate $= 5$
(d) None of these

Question 10.
In which quadrant will the point lie, if the coordinate is 7 and abscissa is -8?
(a) II
(b) III
(c) IV
(d) I

ANSWER KEY

1. (d)	2. (c)	3. (d)	4. (d)	5. (b)	6. (c)	7. (b)	8. (a)	9. (b)	10. (a)

ACTIVITY 11

GRAPH OF LINEAR EQUATION

OBJECTIVE
To obtain a linear equation and draw a graph that represents the linear equation.

MATERIAL REQUIRED
Graph paper, pens, pencil, eraser, ruler.

THEORY
1. Concept of linear equation.
2. To represent the coordinates on the cartesian plane.

PROCEDURE
Let us consider a situation. Suppose you have 60 rupees to spend. You went to a stationery shop to buy some pencils and some pens. The cost of 1 pencil is Rs. 2 and the cost of 1 pen is Rs. 4. Find the number of pencils and pens bought by you from the shop.

1. Construct a linear equation in two variables.
2. Let the number of pencils be x and the number of pens is y.
3. According to the given situation, $60 = 2x + 4y$.
4. Now we have to represent this situation on the graph paper.
5. By taking different values of x, we get different values of y. Put different values of x given in the table to get corresponding values y as shown.

x	0	2	4	6
y	15	14	13	12

6. Take a graph paper and a cartesian system is drawn, i.e., x-axis and y-axis are drawn.
7. Plot the coordinates from the above table on the graph and name them as A(0,15), B(2,14), C(4,13), D(6,12). On joining the points A, B, C and D we get a straight line.

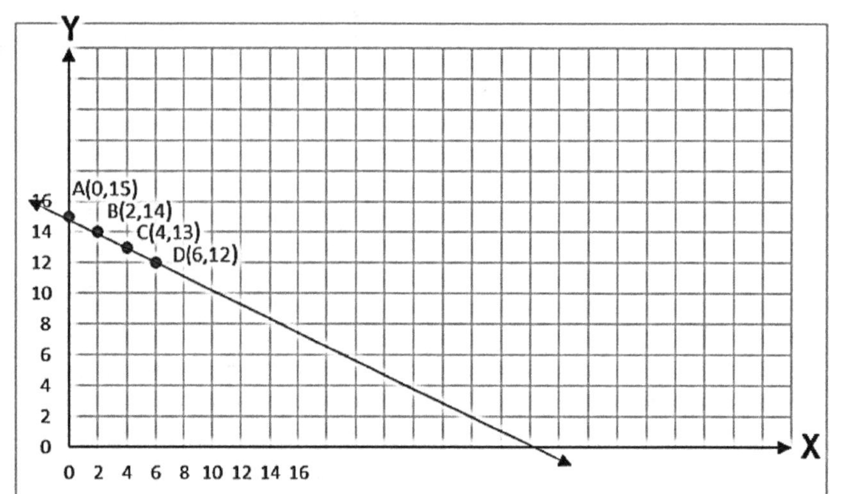

OBSERVATION

1. We get a straight line, which represents the linear equation [fig. (i)].
2. On the line, there are infinitely many coordinates. But, according to the situation we have taken those points or coordinates which are natural numbers.

RESULT

We observed that for the given equation, we get a straight line on the graphpaper which cuts the x-axis and y-axis.

LEARNING OUTCOME

We learnt that for any one-degree equation whether, in one variable or two variables, we will get a straight line on the graph papers. For $x = a$ line is parallel to y-axis at a distance of a unit from origin. For $y = b$, the line will be parallel to x-axis at a distance of b unit from origin.

ACTIVITY TIME

For the other daily life situations, students can draw linear equations on the graph.
For example:

1. $x = 2y$ (cost of one apple is equal to the cost of two oranges).
2. $x + y = 7$ (the sum of some pencils and erasers is 7).

VIVA-VOCE

Question 1. How many solutions will you obtain for $a + b = 3$?
Answer: Infinitely many solutions.

Question 2. How many solutions will you obtain for $3x + 5 = 8$?
Answer: One solution.

Question 3. Write solution of $8x + 4 = 20$.
Answer: 2

Question 4. If $x = 6$, does the equation $x + 6 = 12$ verify?
Answer: Yes.

Question 5. Write the solution for $x = 2$ in $2x + y = 4$.
Answer: (2,0).

Question 6. The cost of a ribbon is thrice the cost of a hair pin. Write this statement in two. variables in a linear equation.
Answer: $x = 3y$, where x is the cost of a ribbon and y is the cost of a hairpin.

Question 7. Write any two solutions of $x = 6y$.
Answer: (0,0) and (6,1).

Question 8. Check whether the point $(-5, -1)$ lies on the line $-3x + y = 12$.
Answer: No, $(-5, -1)$ does not lie on the given line.

Question 9. The solution of equation $x - 2y = 4$ is?
Answer: (4,0)

Question 1.
The value of y at $x = -1$ in the equation $5y = 2$ is
(a) $\frac{5}{2}$
(b) $\frac{2}{5}$
(c) 10
(d) 0

Question 2.
The equation of a line which is 5 units distance above the x-axis is
(a) $x = 5$
(b) $x + 5 = y$
(c) $y - 5$
(d) $x - y = 0$

Question 3.
$x = 3$ and $y = -2$ is a solution of the equation $4px - 3y = 12$, then the value of p is
(a) 0
(b) $\frac{1}{2}$
(c) 2
(d) 3

Question 4.
Which of the following is the equation of a line parallel to y-axis?
(a) $y = 0$
(b) $x + y = z$
(c) $y = x$
(d) $x = a$

Question 5.
Any point on the line $y = 3x$ is of the form
(a) $(a, 3a)$
(b) $(3a, a)$
(c) $\left(a, \frac{a}{3}\right)$
(d) $\left(\frac{a}{3}, -a\right)$

Question 6.
How many linear equations in x and y can be satisfied by $x = 1$ and $y = 2$?
(a) Only one
(b) Two
(c) Infinitely many
(d) Three

Question 7.
Any point of the form $(a, -a)$ always lie on the graph of the equation
(a) $x = -a$
(b) $y = a$
(c) $y = x$
(d) $x + y = 0$

Question 8.
The graph of the equation $2x + 3y = 6$ cuts the x-axis at the point
(a) (0,3)
(b) (3,0)
(c) (2,0)
(d) (0,2)

Question 9.
Graph of linear equation $ax + by + c = 0, a \neq 0, b \neq 0$ cuts x-axis and y-axis respectively at the points.
(a) $\left(\frac{-c}{a}, 0\right), \left(0, \frac{-c}{b}\right)$
(b) $\left(0, \frac{-c}{b}, 0\right), \left(\frac{-c}{a}, 0\right)$
(c) $(-c, 0)(0, -c)$
(d) $(x, 0)(y, 0)$

Question 10.
Which of the following ordered pairs is a solution of the equation $x - 2y - 6$?
(a) (2,4)
(b) (0,3)
(c) (-4,1)
(d) (4,-1)

ANSWER KEY

| 1.(b) | 2.(c) | 3.(b) | 4.(d) | 5.(a) | 6.(a) | 7.(d) | 8.(b) | 9.(a) | 10.(c) |

OBJECTIVE

(A). To find the mid-point of a line segment and the perpendicular bisector of a line segment by using paper folding.

MATERIAL REQUIRED

Tracing papers, geometry box, a pair of scissors.

THEORY

Definition of mid-point and perpendicular bisector.

Definition of Mid-point: A point that divides the line segment into two equal parts is known as a mid-point of a line segment. M is the mid-point of AB.

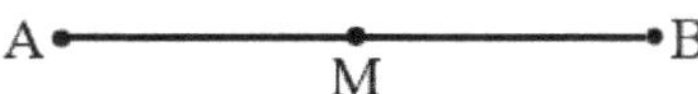

Concept of perpendicular bisector: A-line which is perpendicular to the given line segment and divides into two equal parts is known as the perpendicular bisector of the given line segment.

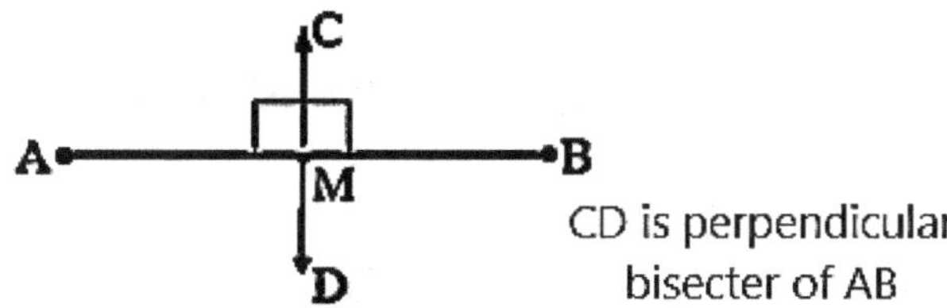

PROCEDURE

1. Take a square sheet of tracing paper and draw a line segment PQ of the desired length as shown in fig. (i).

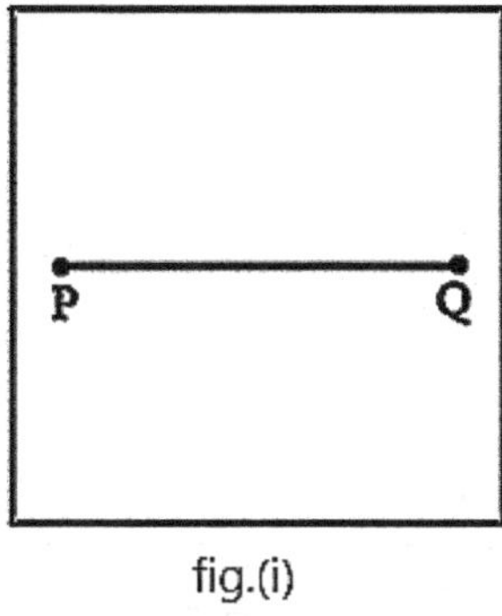

fig.(i)

2. Fold this sheet along the middle in such a way that point P falls on point Q fig.(ii).

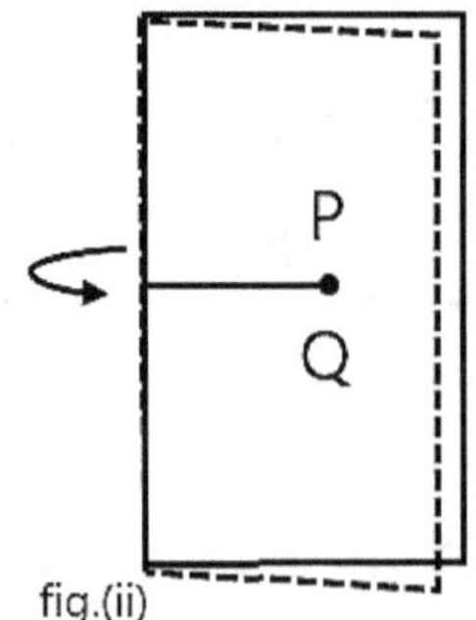

fig.(ii)

3. Press the paper properly, so that a crease is obtained. Unfold the paper and draw the dotted line over the crease.
   Name its AB as shown. Name the point of intersection of line AB and PQ as M fig. (iii).

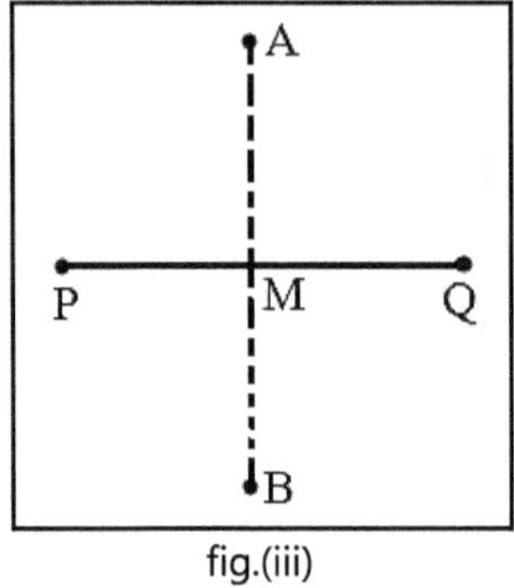

fig.(iii)

OBSERVATION

This point M is the mid-point of line segment PQ and the crease obtained is the perpendicular bisector of PQ.

OBJECTIVE

(B). To draw a perpendicular at a point lying on the line segment and from a point lying outside the line segment.

MATERIAL REQUIRED

Tracing papers, geometry box, a pair of scissors.

PROCEDURE

1. Take a piece of tracing paper and draw a line segment PQ of the desired length as shown in fig.(i).

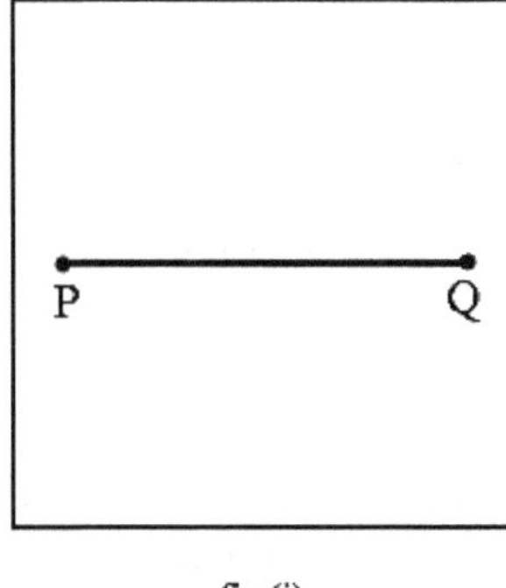

fig.(i)

2. Take any point M on the line segment PQ, now fold the paper in such away that PM falls on MQ as shown in fig.(ii) and fig.(iii) and press the paper.

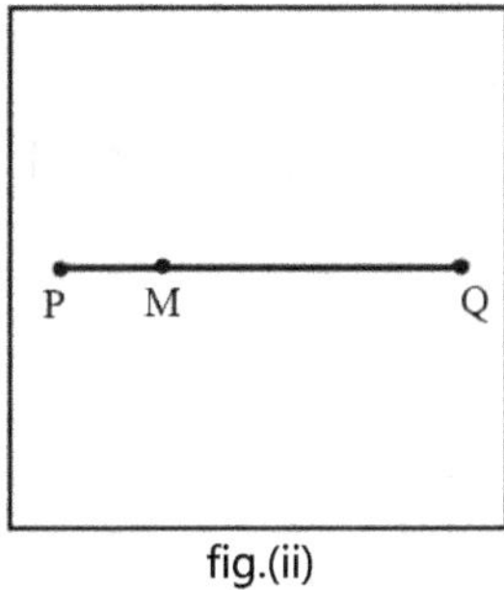

fig.(ii)

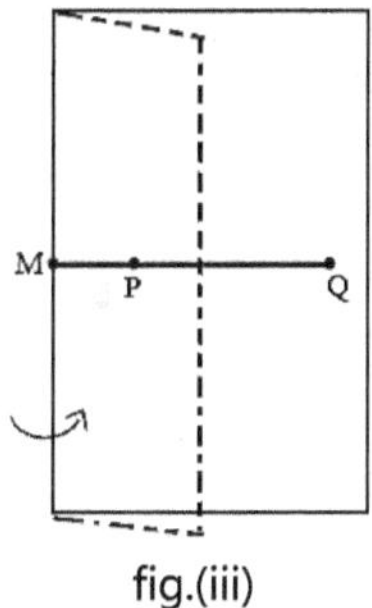

fig.(iii)

3. Open the paper, a crease is formed at M. Draw a dotted line on this crease with pencil and name it as ML.
   In the same way, a perpendicular can be drawn from the point outside the line segment. Hence point M lies outside the line segment PQ.

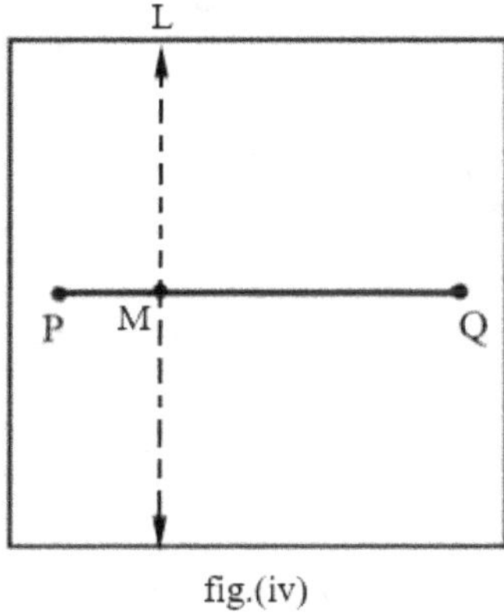

fig.(iv)

4. On tracing paper, draw figure (v) (a) as shown. Fold the paper along line PQ in such a way that its two opposite corners come close together as shown in (b). Press it and mark the image of point M. Name it M', unfold the paper.
5. Join M and M'. MM' is perpendicular to PQ.

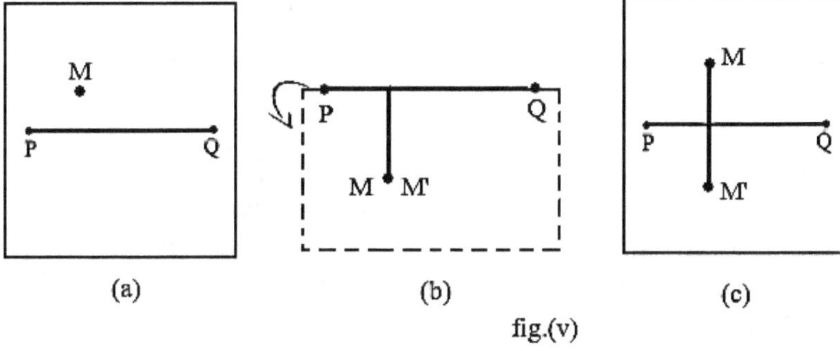

(a)   (b)   (c)

fig.(v)

RESULT

In this way, we find the mid-point of a line segment and perpendicular bisector of a line segment.

LEARNING OUTCOME

By paper folding activity, students will be able to find the mid-point, perpendicular bisector of any line segment and draw a perpendicular from any point lying on or outside the line segment.

1. Take any triangle and draw perpendiculars from the opposite vertex to corresponding side of a triangle.
2. Take any triangle and find the mid-points of three sides by paper folding activity.
3. Take any quadrilateral and find the mid-points of four sides by paper folding activity.

VIVA-VOCE

Question 1. Is it possible to find the mid-point of a line of 9.7 cm with a ruler?
Answer: No. Because the least count of the ruler is 0.1 cm.

Question 2. Which of the following has two end points?
Answer: A line segment

Question 3. If a line segment of length 10 cm is divided by a perpendicular bisector, then what will be the length of each part of the line segment?
Answer: 5 cm.

Question 4. When constructing a line parallel to a given line, you will be?
Answer: copying an angle.

Question 5. What does the word bisect mean?
Answer: To cut something into two congruent pieces or in half.

Question 6. What do you mean by a centroid?
Answer: The centroid is the centre point of the object.

Question 7. Which of the following has a definite length?
Answer. Line segment

MULTIPLE CHOICE QUESTION

Question 1.
Triangle formed by joining the mid-points of an equilateral triangle is a/an:
(a) Right triangle
(b) Isosceles triangle
(c) Equilateral triangle
(d) None of these

Question 2.
A line segment joining mid-points of any two sides in parallel to the third side in the triangle and half in the length of the third side by the theorem of:
(a) Proportionality theorem
(b) Mid-point theorem
(c) Pythagoras theorem
(d) None of these

Question 3.
If M is mid-point of hypotenuse PR of a right-angled triangle PQR right-angled at Q then :
(a) $MP = MR$
(b) $MQ = MR$
(c) $MQ = MP$
(d) All of $(a), (b), (c)$

Question 4.
The figure formed by joining the mid-points of the sides of a quadrilateral ABCD, taken in order, is a square only if,
(a) ABCD is a rhombus
(b) Diagonals of ABCD are equal
(c) Diagonals of ABCD are equal and perpendicular
(d) Diagonals of ABCD are perpendicular

Question 5.
D and E are the mid-points of the sides AB and AC respectively of $\triangle$ ABC. DE is produced to F. To prove that CF is equal and parallel to OA, we need an additional:
(a) $\angle DAE = \angle EFC$
(b) $AE = EF$
(c) $DE = EF$
(d) $\angle ADE = \angle ECF$

Question 6.
The quadrilateral formed by joining the mid-points of the sides of a quadrilateral PQRS, taken in order, is a rectangle, if:
(a) PQRS is a rectangle
(b) PQRS is a parallelogram
(c) Diagonals of PQRS are equal
(d) Diagonals of PQRS are equal

Question 7.
The figure obtained by joining the mid-points of the sides of a rhombus, taken in order is:
(a) A rhombus
(b) A rectangle
(c) A square
(d) Any parallelogram

Question 8.
D and E are the mid-points of the sides AB and AC of $\triangle$ ABC and O is any point on side BC. O is joined to A. If P and Q are the mid-points of OB and OC respectively, then $\triangle$ EQP is:
(a) A square
(b) A rectangle
(c) A rhombus
(d) A parallelogram

Question 9.
Quadrilateral formed by joining the mid-points of any quadrilateral is always:
(a) Rectangle
(b) Square
(c) Rhombus
(d) Parallelogram

Question 10.
In a $\triangle$ ABC, AB = 3 cm, BC = 4 cm and A = 5 cm. If D and E are mid-points of AB and BC respectively, then the length of DE is:
(a) 1.5 cm
(b) 2 cm
(c) 2.5 cm
(d) 3.5 cm

ANSWER KEY

1. (c)	2. (b)	3. (d)	4. (c)	5. (c)	6. (c)	7. (b)	8. (d)	9. (d)	10. (a)

OBJECTIVE

To divide a line segment into equal parts.

MATERIAL REQUIRED

A sheet of ruled paper in which all the lines are parallel and equidistant,tracing paper or transparent sheet, geometry box.

THEORY

Intercept Theorem: If there are three (or more) parallel lines and intercepts made by them on any transversal are equal, then intercepts made by them on any other transversal are also equal.

PROCEDURE

1. Take a piece of tracing paper sheet and draw a line segment of length 10 cm or 9 cm (let line segment is to be divided into 7 equal parts). Name it as PQ.

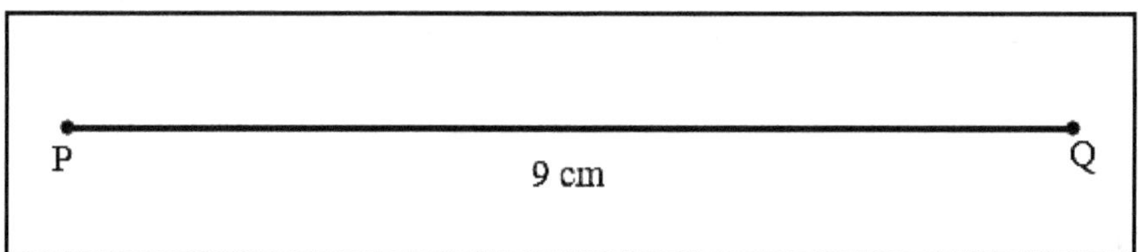

2. Now, take a ruled sheet, and mark the lines as 0, 1, 2, 3, 4...10 from top to bottom.
3. Place the paper strip (tracing paper) on the ruled sheet such that the point P coincides as with the line (ruled sheet) marked 0, and another point Q coincides with the line marked 7 as shown in fig.(i).
4. Mark the points on PQ which are the points of intersection with lines of a ruled sheet as A_1, A_2, A_3,...........A_6.
5. Now remove the ruled sheet.

OBSERVATION

7 equal parts will be obtained.

$PA_1 = A_1A_2 = A_2A_3 = A_3A_4 = A_4A_5 = A_5A_6 = A_6Q$.

Here, marked axis PQ is a transversal on parallel lines of the ruled sheet with equal intercept. Therefore, PQ also has equal intercepts (By intercept theorem).

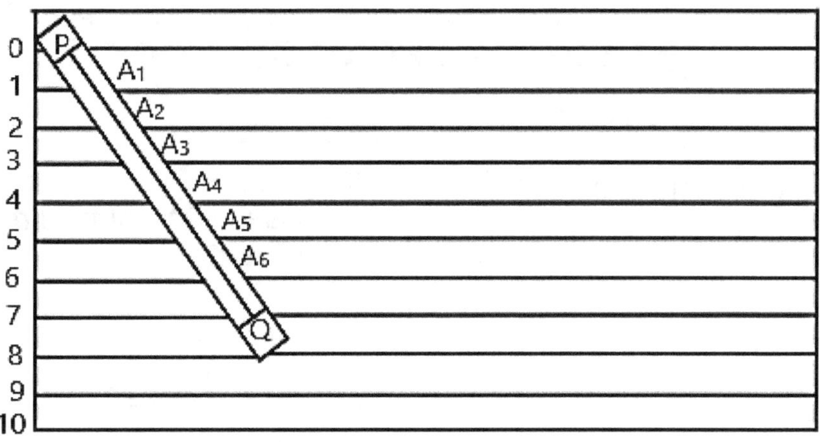

RESULT

Line PQ is divided into 7 equal parts.

LEARNING OUTCOME

By paper activity, a line segment of any measurement can be divided into equal parts.

ACTIVITY TIME

1. Draw a line segment of 7 cm and divide it into 6 equal parts and draw perpendicular on the 4th point of a line segment, by paper folding.
2. Take any rectangular sheet of 5 cm by 9 cm and divide the edges of a sheet into 8 equal parts.
3. Take any rectangular sheet of 10 cm by 7 cm and divide along the length in 10 equal parts and along with the breadth in 7 equal parts (By paper folding).

VIVA-VOCE

Question 1. Define parallel lines.
Answer: Two lines in a plane are said to be parallel lines if they do not have a common point i.e., they do not intersect.

Question 2. Define parallel rays.
Answer: Two rays in the same plane are parallel if they do not intersect each other even if extended indefinitely beyond their initial points.

Question 3. Define parallel line segments.
Answer: Two-line segments are parallel if the corresponding line segments determined by them are parallel.

Question 4. To divide a thread in 10 equal parts, how many successive folds will you give?
Answer: 9 folds.

Question 5. Define intercept theorem?
Answer: The Intercept theorem provides the ratios between the line segments created when two parallel lines are intercepted by two intersecting lines.

Question 6. Define transversal line.
Answer: A-line intersecting two or more given lines in a plane at different points is called a transversal to the given lines.

Question 7. Write any four examples of parallel line segments.
Answer: The four examples are the opposite edges of a plain paper, the opposite edges of a black board, the opposite edges of a scale, railway lines.

MULTIPLE CHOICE QUESTION

Question 1:
Write first two equivalent fractions of $\frac{3}{5}$

(a) $\frac{5}{2}, \frac{10}{2}$

(b) $\frac{10}{4}, \frac{15}{6}$

(c) $\frac{6}{10}, \frac{9}{15}$

(d) None of these

Question 2.
If $Q = 12$ cm, is divided into three equal parts, what is the ratio of first two parts to the remaining part?
(a) $2:1$
(b) $1:1$
(c) $3:2$
(d) None of these

Question 3.
Find x, if $\frac{10}{9} = \frac{30}{x}$
(a) 30
(b) 27
(c) 25
(d) None of these

Question 4.
The length of a line segment is 24 cm, what is the length of each part, if it is divided into 10 equal parts?
(a) 1.2 cm
(b) 2.5 cm
(c) 2.4 cm
(d) None of these

Question 5.
If $\frac{8}{5} = \frac{x}{25}$ what is the value of x ?
(a) 35
(b) 40
(c) 15
(d) None of these

Question 6.
If $Q = 20$ cm, is divided into four equal parts, what is the ratio of the first two parts to the whole part?
(a) $1:1$
(b) $2:1$
(c) $1:2$
(d) None of these

Question 7.
In the given figure, lines l and m will be parallel, if angle x will be equal to

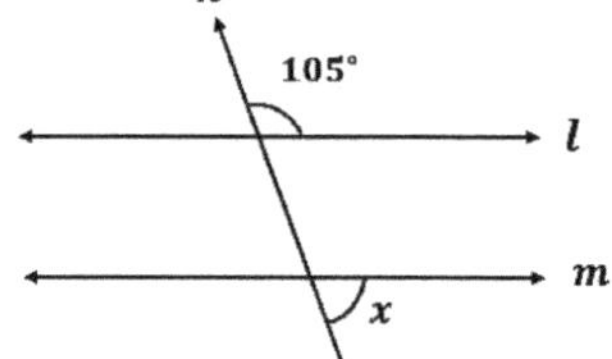

(a) $65°$
(b) $50°$
(c) $15°$
(d) $75°$

Question 8.
The following diagram shows two parallel lines cut by a transversal. What is the measure of $\angle 2$?

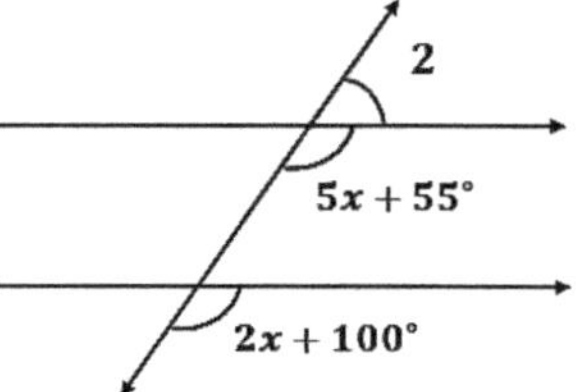

(a) $15°$
(b) $75°$
(c) $50°$
(d) $80°$

Question 9.
If two interior angles on the same side of a transversal intersecting two parallel lines are in the ratio $2:3$, then the greater of the two angles is
(a) $54°$
(b) $108°$
(c) $120°$
(d) $136°$

ANSWER KEY

1.(a)	2.(b)	3.(a)	4.(a)	5.(b)	6.(c)	7.(d)	8.(a)	9.(d)

DIVISION OF A PAPER STRIP IN EQUAL PARTS

OBJECTIVE
To divide a thin strip of paper into equal parts (7 equal parts).

MATERIAL REQUIRED
Tracing sheet, colours, ruled sheet of paper, geometry box.

THEORY
Intercept Theorem: If there are three (or more) parallel lines and intercepts made by them on any transversal are equal, then intercepts made by them on any other transversal are also equal.

PROCEDURE
1. Cut a rectangular strip of paper from a tracing sheet which is to be divided into 7 equal parts. Name it as ABCD.

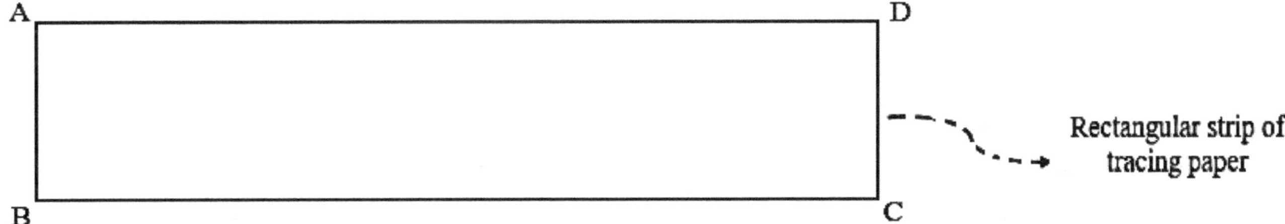

2. Now, take a ruled sheet, and mark the lines as 0, 1, 2, 3, 4 from top to bottom.
3. Place the paper strip on the ruled sheet such as the point A coincides with the line marked 0 and the point D coincides with the line marked 7 as shown in the fig. (ii).

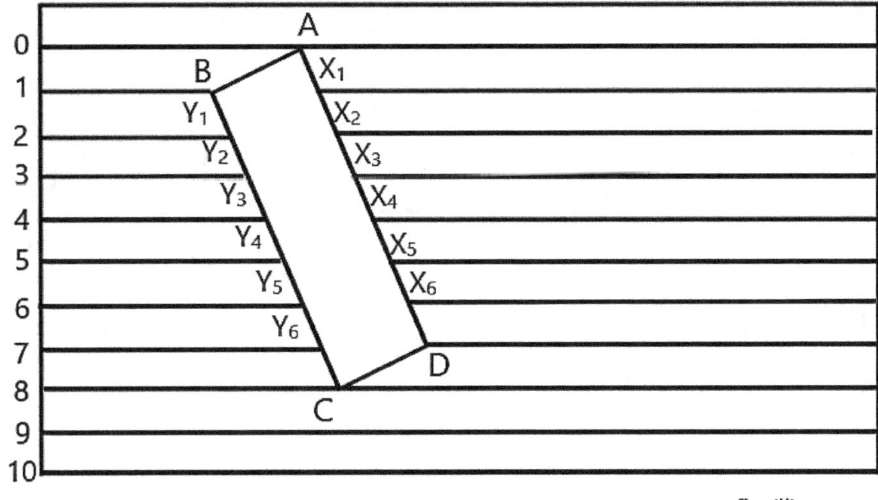

fig.(ii)

4. Mark the points on the strip where parallel lines of ruled sheet cut the strip as X_1, X_2, X_3, X_4, X_5, X_6 on line AD and Y_1, Y_2, Y_3, Y_4, Y_5, Y_6 on line BC.

5. Now draw the lines X_1Y_1, X_2Y_2, X_3Y_3, X_4Y_4, X_5Y_5, X_6Y_6, parallel to AB and colour them as shown in fig. (iii).

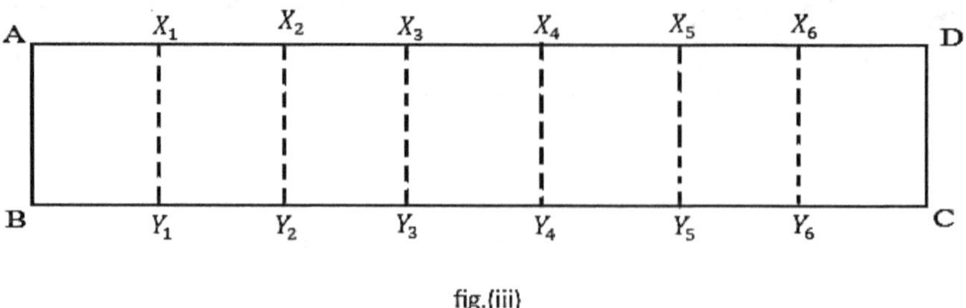

fig.(iii)

OBSERVATION

X_1Y_1, X_2Y_2, X_3Y_3, X_4Y_4, X_5Y_5, X_6Y_6 divide the paper strip into seven equal parts.

RESULT

We obtain an equally divided strip as $AX_1Y_1B=X_1X_2Y_2Y_1=X_2X_3Y_3Y_2=X_3X_4Y_4Y_3=X_4X_5Y_5Y_4=X_5X_6Y_6Y_5=X_6DCY_6$.

LEARNING OUTCOME

Students can divide any rectangular strip into equal parts.

ACTIVITY TIME

To make a fraction chart.

1. Take 9 strips of the same size and colour them with different colours.

2. Now by using a ruled sheet, divide these strips into 1, 2, 3, 4, 5, 6,......9 equal parts.

3. Paste these divided strips on a chart paper one below the other. See fig.(iv).

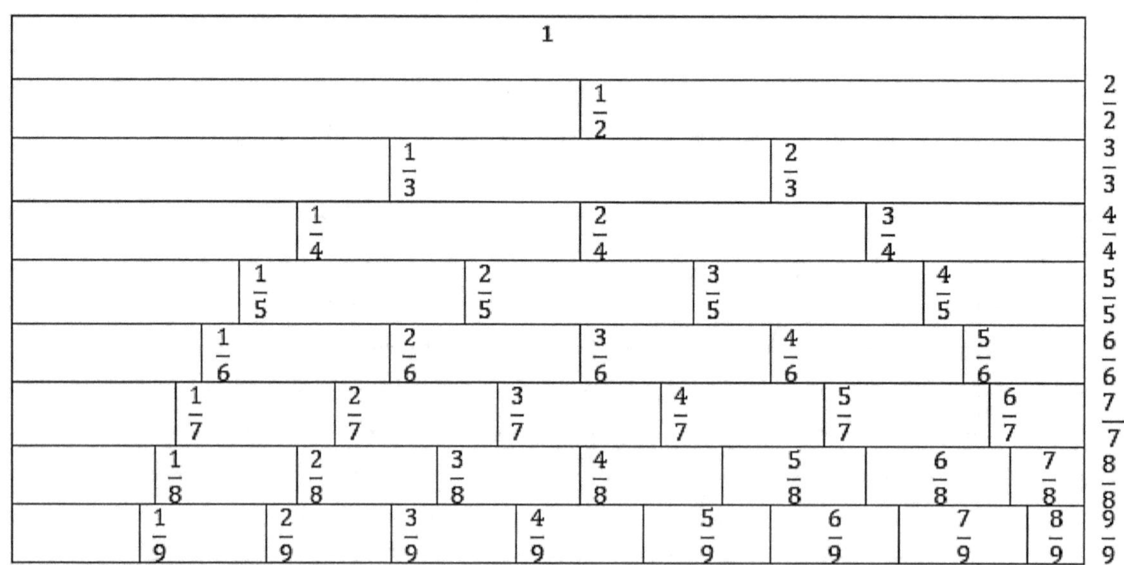

Fraction Chart   fig(iv)

4. A beautiful fraction chart is formed. Students may use different colour-glazed papers to make them attractive and to identify clearly.

Question 1. What is $\frac{1}{5}$ th of a rectangular strip?
Answer: A strip is divided into five equal parts; each part is one-fifth.

Question 2. What are parallel lines?
Answer: Parallel lines can be defined as two lines in the same plane that are at equal distance from each other and never meet.

Question 3. If a strip is divided into 9 equal parts what will be the value of 7 parts?
Answer: $\frac{7}{9}$.

Question 4: What is the perimeter of square?
Answer: $4a$.

Question 5. If a strip is divided into 5 equal parts what will be the value of 2 parts?
Answer: $\frac{2}{5}$.

Question 6. Can you divide a strip of 11 cm, into 6 equal parts by using a ruler?
Answer: No.

Question 7. Can you divide a strip of 12 cm, into 6 equal parts by using a ruler?
Answer: Yes.

Question 8. How many folds are required to divide a rope into 20 equal parts?
Answer: 19 folds.

MULTIPLE CHOICE QUESTION

Question 1.
What is the length of one part of the strip of 12 cm, if it is divided into two equal parts?
(a) 8 cm
(b) $\frac{2}{7}$ cm
(c) 6 cm
(d) None of these

Question 2.
What will be the value of 8 parts of a strip if it is divided into 12 equal parts?
(a) $\frac{1}{9}$
(b) $\frac{7}{12}$
(c) $\frac{8}{12}$
(d) None of these

Question 3.
If a rectangular strip of 20 cm is divided into 10 equal parts, what will be the length of each part?
(a) 2 cm
(b) 1 cm
(c) 3 cm
(d) None of these

Question 4.
What is the equivalent fraction of $\frac{4}{5}$?
(a) $\frac{8}{10}$
(b) $\frac{6}{25}$
(c) $\frac{3}{2}$
(d) None of these

Question 5.
Write two equivalent fractions of $\frac{8}{9}$?
(a) $\frac{10}{12}, \frac{15}{18}$
(b) $\frac{16}{18}, \frac{24}{27}$
(c) $\frac{6}{5}, \frac{10}{12}$
(d) None of these

Question 6.
To divide a thread into 16 equal parts, how many successive folds will you give?
(a) 15
(b) 16
(c) 17
(d) None of these

Question 7.
Which is greater $\left(\frac{46}{30}\right)$ or $\left(\frac{17}{5}\right)$?
(a) $\frac{46}{30}$
(b) $\frac{17}{5}$
(c) $\frac{16}{29}$
(d) None of these

Question 8.
Write two fractions which is equal to 2.
(a) $\frac{4}{4}, \frac{6}{6}$
(b) $\frac{6}{4}, \frac{5}{3}$
(c) $\frac{18}{9}, \frac{24}{12}$
(d) None of these

Question 9.
Add: $2\frac{5}{3} + 7\frac{5}{6}$
(a) $\frac{23}{2}$
(b) $\frac{48}{15}$
(c) $\frac{6}{7}$
(d) None of these

Question 10.
Simplify: $\frac{2}{11} + \frac{8}{3} - \frac{7}{33}$
(a) $\frac{11}{90}$
(b) $\frac{87}{33}$
(c) $\frac{22}{50}$
(d) None of these

ANSWER KEY

1.(c)	2.(b)	3.(a)	4.(a)	5.(b)	6.(a)	7.(b)	8.(c)	9.(a)	10.(b)

RELATIONS OF INEQUALITIES IN TRIANGLE

OBJECTIVE

To verify that a triangle is possible only if the sum of any two sides of triangleis always greater than the third side and difference of any two sides is always less than the third side.

MATERIAL REQUIRED

Broom sticks or straws, scale, geometry box.

THEORY

1. Measurement of line segments.
2. Comparison of line segments.

PROCEDURE

1. Take some sticks according to the given measurements.
2. Collect three triplets of sticks as given.

SET I

- 3cm, 5cm, 10cm

- 4cm, 4cm, 8cm

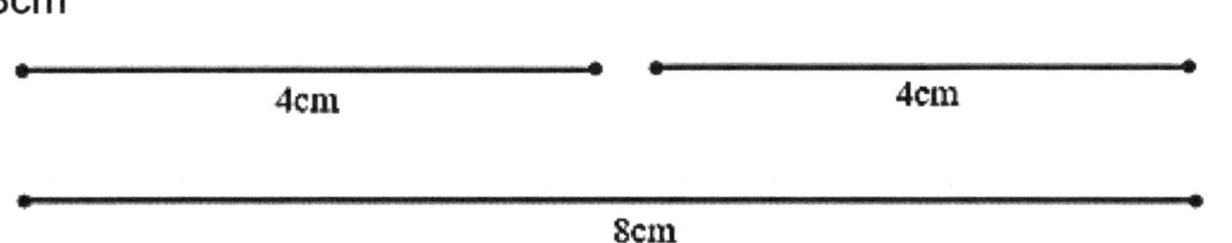

- 5cm, 4cm, 8cm

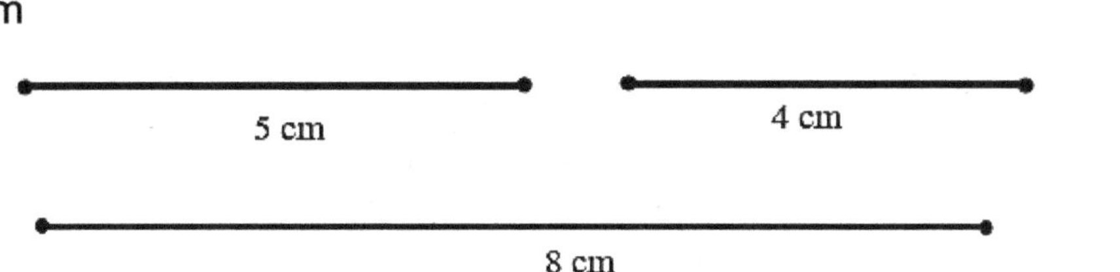

SET II

- 3cm, 4cm, 8cm

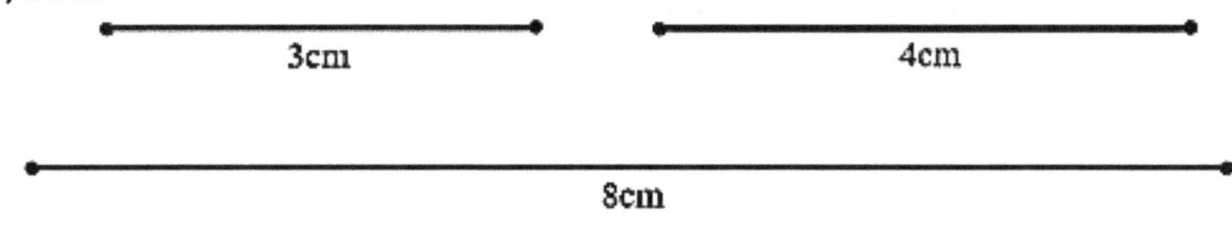

- 4cm, 6cm, 10cm

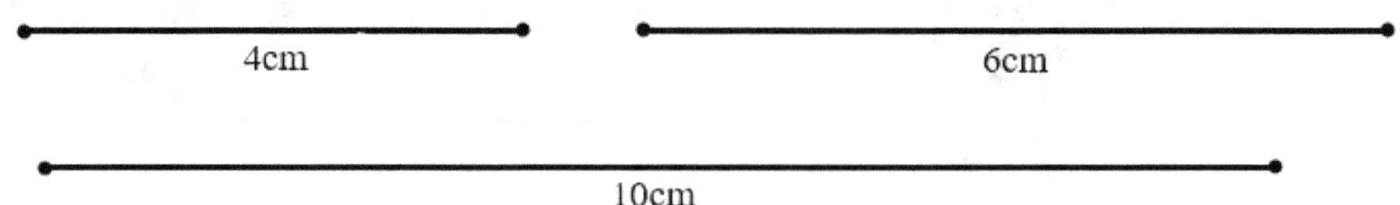

- 4cm, 5cm, 7cm

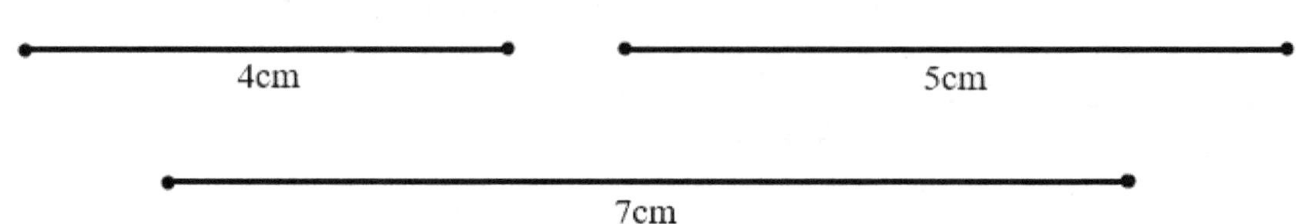

SET III

- 5cm, 3cm, 6cm

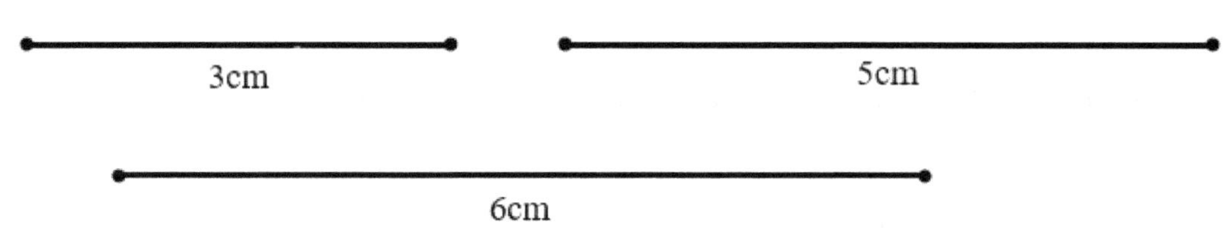

- 5cm, 5cm, 11cm

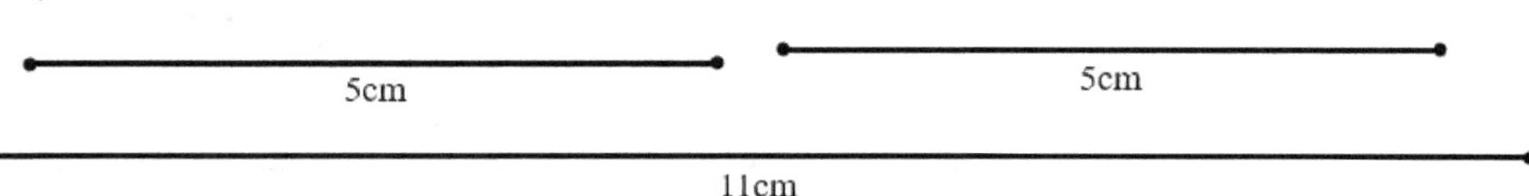

- 3cm, 2cm, 5cm

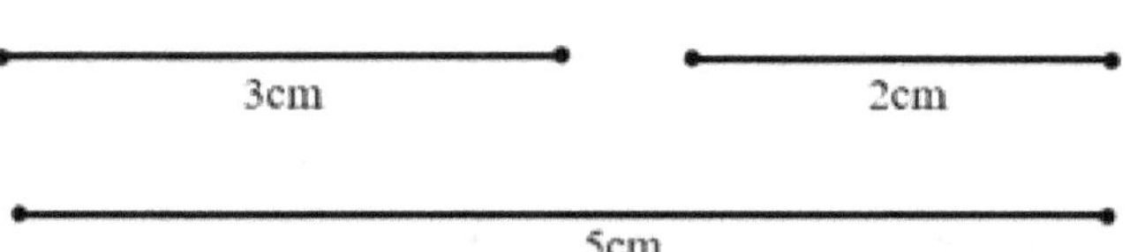

3. Now from the above three sets, try to form a triangle and name them.

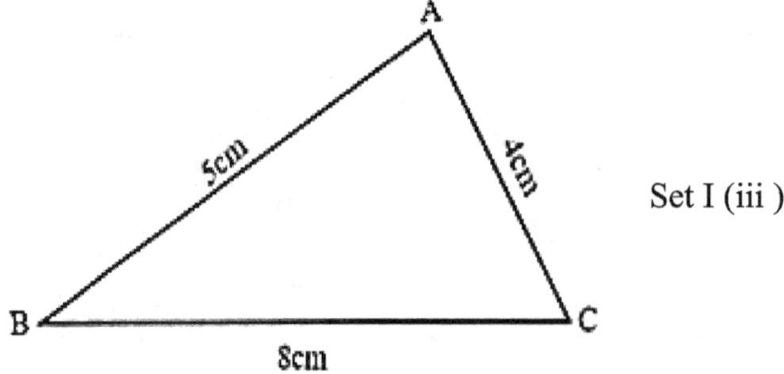

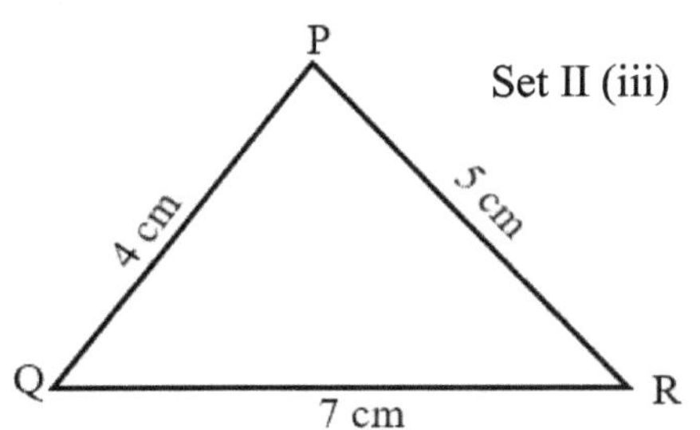

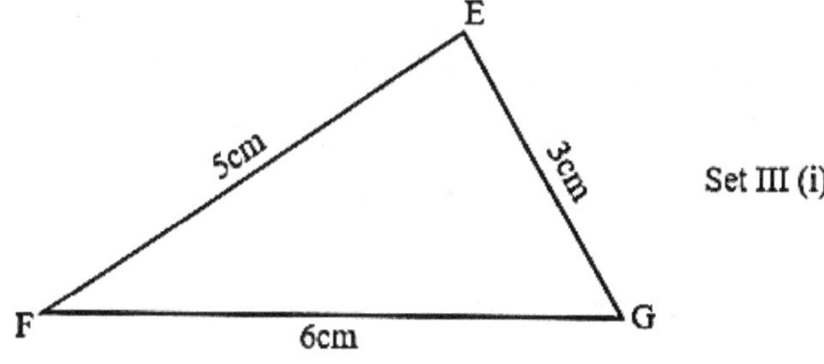

OBSERVATION AND CALCULATION TABLE

Set		Side 1	Side 2	Side 3	Possibility of Δ	Reason
I						
	(i)	3	5	10	not possible	$3 + 5 < 10$
	(ii)	4	4	8	not possible	$4 + 4 = 8$
	(iii)	5	4	8	possible	$5 + 4 > 8$ $5 + 8 > 4$ $4 + 8 > 5$
II						
	(i)	3	4	8	not possible	$3 + 4 < 8$
	(ii)	4	6	10	not possible	$4 + 6 = 10$
	(iii)	4	5	7	possible	$4 + 5 > 7$ $5 + 7 > 4$ $4 + 7 > 5$
III						
	(i)	5	3	6	possible	$5 + 3 > 6$ $5 + 6 > 3$ $3 + 6 > 5$
	(ii)	5	5	11	not possible	$5 + 5 < 11$
	(iii)	3	2	5	not possible	$3 + 2 = 5$

In each set, we observe that triangle is possible only when the sum of the two sides is greater than the third side.

RESULT
We verified that the triangle is possible only when the sum of any two sides is greater than the third side.

LEARNING OUTCOME
We learnt that, for any three-line segments, we cannot construct a triangle always because for a triangle the sum of any two sides of a triplet is always greater than the third side.

ACTIVITY TIME
1. For a triplet, verify that the difference of any two sides is always less than the third side in a

triangle.
   2. Are the following triangles possible?
      - Right-angled equilateral triangle.
      - Obtuse equilateral triangle.
      - All angles are acute angle.
   3. Two obtuse angles in a triangle.

VIVA-VOCE

Question 1. What is an equilateral triangle?
Answer: Equilateral triangle - having all sides equal.

Question 2. What is the sum of an interior angle of a triangle?
Answer: 180°

Question 3. State, if the following triangles are possible: (a) 8cm, 6cm, 11cm
          (b) 6cm, 7cm, 13cm,
Answer: (a) Yes   (b) No.

Question 4. What is an isosceles triangle?
Answer: Isosceles triangle - having any two equal sides

Question 5. In an equilateral triangle each angle of
Answer: 60°

Question 6. In an acute angle triangle, each angle of?
Answer: Less than 90°

Question 7. What do you mean by line segment?
Answer: A part of a line that is bounded by two distinct end points.

Question 8. Is it possible to construct a triangle with sides 4cm, 5cm and 7 cm?
Answer: Yes

MULTIPLE CHOICE QUESTION

Question 1.
Is the obtuse right triangle possible?
(a) No
(b) Yes
(c) Can't say
(d) None of these

Question 2.
If the semi-perimeter of an equilateral triangle
is $28\sqrt{3}$ cm, then its area is
(a) $784\sqrt{3}$ cm²
(b) $684\sqrt{2}$ cm²
(c) $\frac{784\sqrt{3}}{3}$ cm²
(d) $\frac{684\sqrt{3}}{3}$ cm²

Question 3.
Two sides of a triangle are of lengths 5 cm and 1.5 cm. The length of the third side of the triangle cannot be:
(a) 3.6 cm
(b) 4.1 cm
(c) 3.8 cm
(d) 3.4 cm

Question 4.
In triangles ABC and PQR, AB = AC, $\angle C = \angle P$ and $\angle B = \angle Q$. The two triangles are
(a) Isosceles but not congruent.
(b) Isosceles but congruent.
(c) Congruent but not isosceles.
(d) Neither congruent nor isosceles.

Question 5.
In a $\triangle ABC$, $\angle A = 85°$, $\angle B = 65°$, what will be the least side of $\triangle ABC$?
(a) AB
(b) BC
(c) AC
(d) None of these

Question 6.
In the given figure, the ratio
$\angle ABD : \angle ACD$ is
(a) $1:1$
(b) $2:1$
(c) $1:2$
(d) None of these

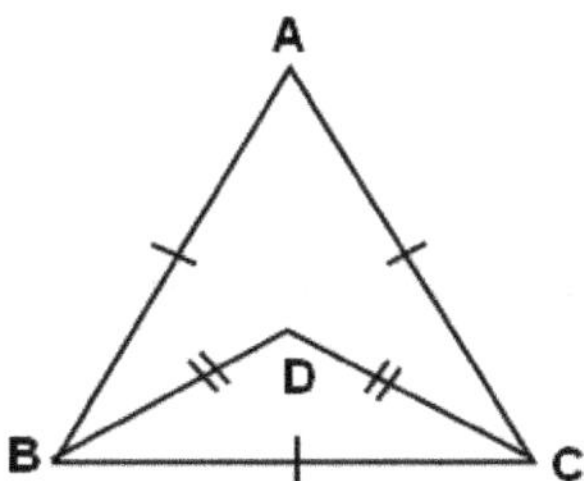

Question 7.
Which is the longest side in a right-angled triangle?
(a) Altitude
(b) Base
(c) Hypotenuse
(d) None of these

Question 8.
In a scalene triangle
(a) difference of two sides is greater than the third side
(c) the sum of two sides is greater than the third side
(b) product of two sides is greater than the third side
(d) None of these

Question 9.
The three values of angles are $65°$, $85°$, $30°$. Is the triangle possible by using these angles?
(a) Right triangle
(b) Yes
(c) No
(d) None of these

ANSWER KEY

1. (c)	2. (c)	3. (d)	4. (a)	5. (a)	6. (a)	7. (c)	8. (c)	9. (b)

OBJECTIVE
To obtain a parallelogram by paper folding, whose adjacent sides are given.

MATERIAL REQUIRED
Glazed papers, pen, pencil, scale.

THEORY
1. A parallelogram is a quadrilateral in which the pairs of opposite sides are equal and parallel.
2. Basic properties of a parallelogram.

PROCEDURE
1. Take a sheet of glazed paper. Draw any two intersecting rays AB and BC such that they form an acute angle which will be the two adjacent sides of a parallelogram.

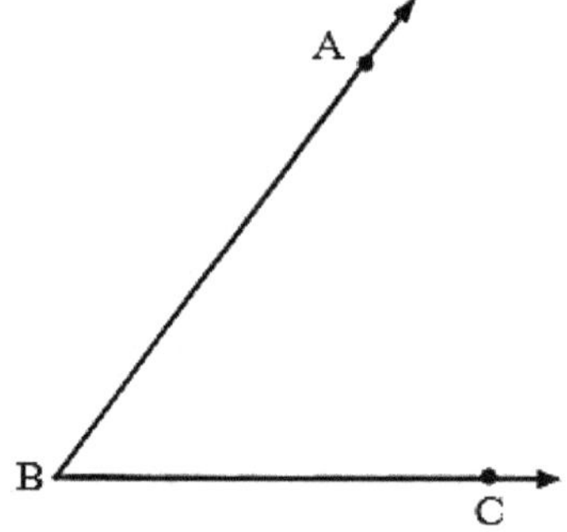

2. Fold the paper along a line that cuts the line BC, the part of line BC that lies on one side of the line of fold falls on the other part. Make a crease, such that $X_1Y_1 \perp BC$ and unfold the paper.

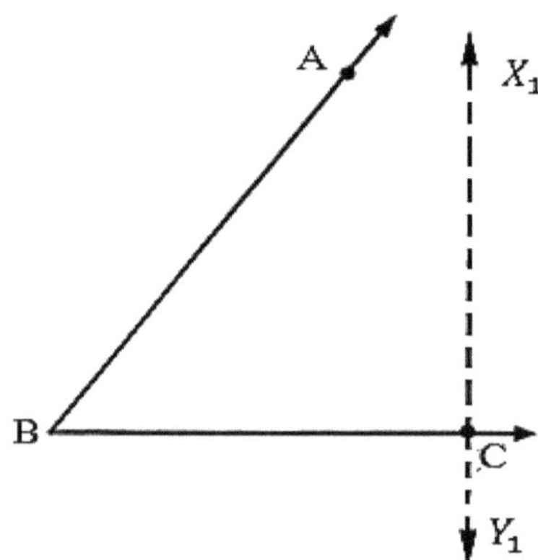

3. Fold the paper such that line passes through point A and is parallel to BC. Make a crease and unfold the paper. Draw the dotted line X_2Y_2.

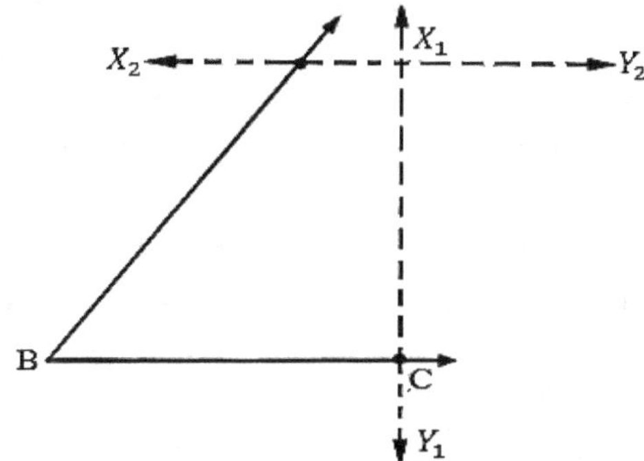

4. Fold the paper along the line that passes through the point C which is parallel to line AB and cuts the line X_2Y_2. Make a crease and unfold it. Draw the line parallel to AB. Mark the intersecting point of X_2Y_2 and X_3Y_3 as D.

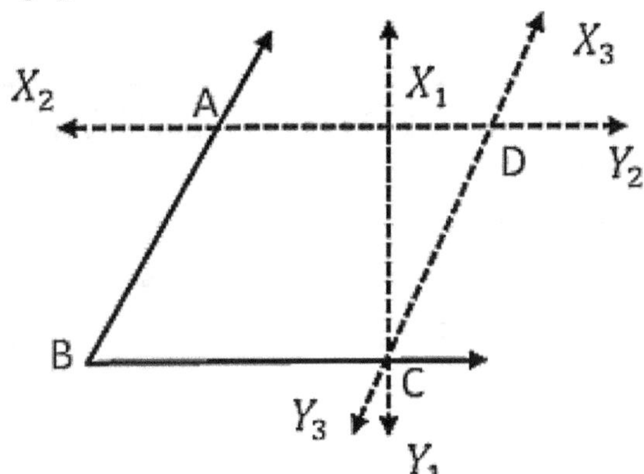

OBSERVATION
Since AD is parallel to BC and DC is parallel to AB, ABCD is the required parallelogram

RESULT
ABCD is the required parallelogram having AB and BC as its two adjacent sides.

LEARNING OUTCOME
Without using protector and scale, we can construct a parallelogram by paper folding of any measurement.

ACTIVITY TIME
Students may construct a parallelogram of sides 4cm and 6cm with different angles.

Question 1. What is the relationship between the areas of the parallelograms on the same base (or equal bases) and between the same parallel lines? **Answer:** Both areas are same.	**Question 2.** What are the types of parallelograms? **Answer:** Parallelograms are of three types, i.e., rectangle, square, and rhombus.

Question 3. How would you define the area of a parallelogram?
Answer: The area of a parallelogram is the product of its base and the corresponding altitude.

Question 4. What is the altitude of a parallelogram?
Answer: Altitude of a parallelogram is the perpendicular distance between two parallel sides.

Question 5. Is it correct that the diagonals of a parallelogram bisect the angles?
Answer: Yes.

Question 6. Is it correct that every square and rhombus are parallelograms?
Answer: Yes, because opposite sides of their figures are parallel and equal.

Question 7. In which quadrilateral figure diagonals are not equal other than parallelogram?
Answer: Rhombus.

Question 8. Do the diagonals of a parallelogram divide it into two triangles of equal base?
Answer: No, the diagonals of a parallelogram divide it into four triangles of equal base.

MULTIPLE CHOICE QUESTION

Question 1.
The quadrilateral formed by joining the mid-points of the sides of a quadrilateral PQRS taken in order is a rhombus, if
(a) PQRS is a rhombus.
(b) PQRS is a paralellogram.
(c) Diagonals of PQRS are perpendicular.
(d) Diagonals of PQRS are equal.

Question 2.
If Diagonals AC and BD of a quadrilateral ABCD intersect at O in such a way that ar($\triangle$ AOD) = ar($\triangle$ BOC). Then ABCD is a:
(a) Parallelogram
(b) Rectangle
(c) Square
(d) Trapezium

Question 3.
The figure obtained by joining the mid-points of the sides of a rhombus taken in order is
(a) A rhombus
(b) A rectangle
(c) A square
(d) Any parallelogram

Question 4.
In a trapezium $ABCD$ with $AB \parallel CD$ and $AD = BC$, if $\angle D = 70°$, then $\angle C$ will be of
(a) 70°
(b) 110°
(c) 20°
(d) None of these

Question 5.
Points D and E are the mid-points of sides AB and AC of a $\triangle$ ABC. If the length of line segment DE = 6.5 cm, then length of side BC is equal to
(a) 6.5 cm
(b) 26 cm
(c) 13 cm
(d) 5.5 cm

Question 6.
The ratio of the line segment joining the mid-points of any two sides of a triangle and the third side is given by
(a) 2 : 1
(b) 1 : 2
(c) 1 : 1
(d) 2 : 3

Question 7.
D and E are the mid-points of the sides AB and AC respectively of $\triangle$ ABC and O is any point on side BC. O is joined to A. If P and Q are the mid-points of OB and OC respectively, then DEQP is
(a) a square
(b) a rectangle

(c) a rhombus
(d) a parallelogram

Question 8.
The area of the figure formed by joining the mid-points of the adjacent sides of a rhombus with diagonals 12 cm and 16 cm is
(a) 48 cm^2
(b) 96 cm^2
(c) 64 cm^2
(d) 192 cm^2

Question 9.
find the perimeter of parallelogram if

$AB = CD = 10cm, AD = BC = 25$
(a) 85 cm
(b) 75 cm
(c) 70 cm
(d) 65 cm

Question 10.
Parallelogram is a
(a) Pentagon
(b) Quadrilateral
(c) Heptagon
(d) Octagon

ANSWER KEY

1.(d)	2.(d)	3.(b)	4.(a)	5.(c)	6.(b)	7.(d)	8.(a)	9.(c)	10.(b)

OBJECTIVE

To show that the quadrilateral formed by joining the mid-points of the adjacent sides of a quadrilateral is a parallelogram by paper folding.

MATERIAL REQUIRED

Glazed papers, pencil, a pair of scissors, glue stick and tracing paper.

THEORY

1. Concept of finding mid-point of a line segment by performing a paper folding activity.
2. Properties of a parallelogram.

PROCEDURE

1. Take any coloured glazed paper.
2. Draw a quadrilateral of any dimensions on glazed paper and name it as ABCD.
3. Cut that quadrilateral from the glazed paper.
4. Now, find the mid-point of each side AB, BC, CD, DA by paper folding and name them E, F, G, H respectively as shown in fig.(i).

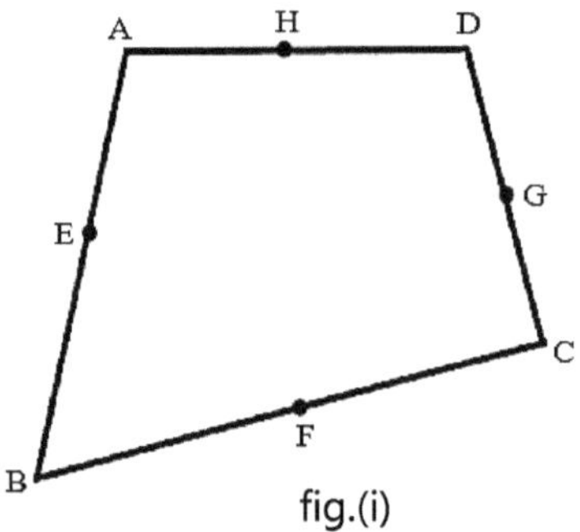

fig.(i)

5. Now, fold the figure along with EF, GF, GH and EH. Press it and then unfold it as shown in fig. (ii).

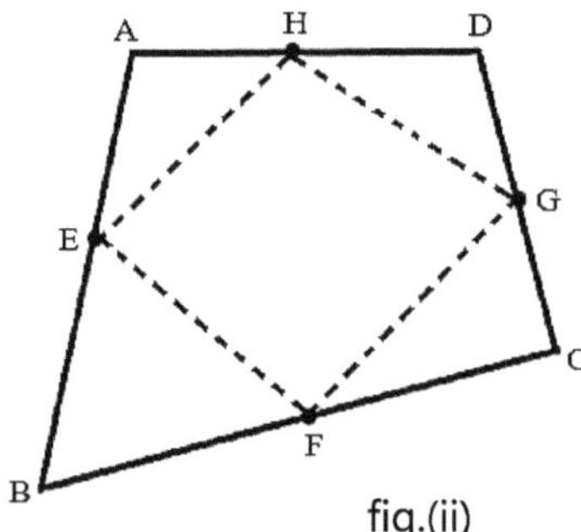

fig.(ii)

6. We will get creases along with EF, GF, GH, HE.
7. Make a replica (true copy) of EFGH (say PQRS) by using tracing paper fig.(iii)

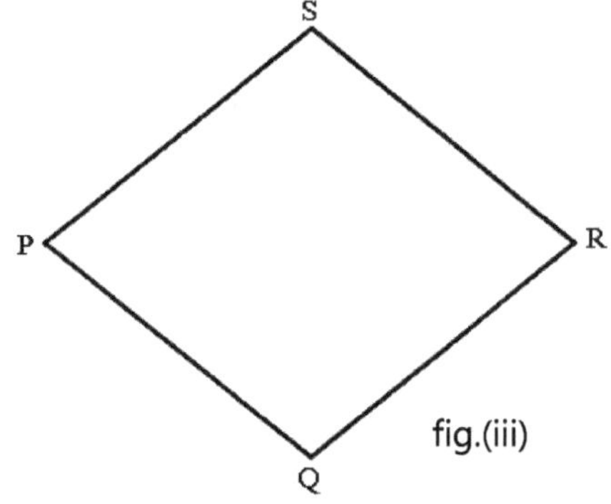

fig.(iii)

8. Cut the quadrilateral PQRS along any diagonal (say RP) [fig.(iv)].

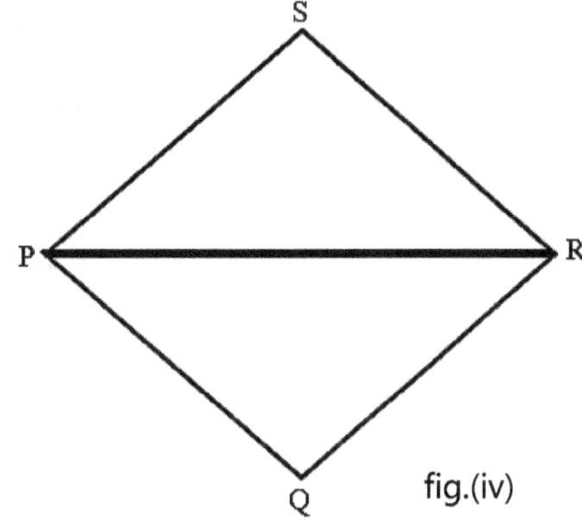

fig.(iv)

9. We will get two triangles ΔPSR and ΔPQR.
10. Now, overlap these two triangles. Two triangles coincide with each other[fig.(v)] such that side PS overlaps with QR and PQ with SR.

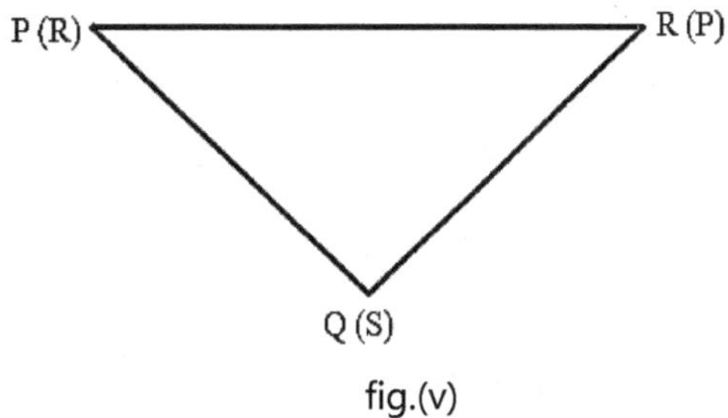

fig.(v)

OBSERVATION

We observe that two triangles coincide with each other which means two triangles are congruent to each other. In a quadrilateral, two triangles cover each other completely along any diagonal, then the quadrilateral will be a parallelogram.

∴ $\qquad\triangle PQR = \triangle PSR$

i.e., $\qquad ar(\triangle PQR) = ar(\triangle PSR)$

∴ PQRS is a parallelogram.

RESULT

As the replica of ΔPQR exactly covers the replica of ΔPSR

∴ $\qquad PQ = RS, \qquad QR = SP$

∴ PQRS is a parallelogram.

We have verified by paper folding that the quadrilateral formed by joining mid-points of adjacent sides of a quadrilateral will be a parallelogram. We also learnt that a diagonal always divides the parallelogram into two triangles of equal areas.

What type of figures do you obtain?
1. If you join mid-points of the sides of a rectangle (Do it by paper folding).
2. If you join the mid-points of the sides of a square (Do it by paper folding).

VIVA-VOCE

Question 1. Name the quadrilateral in which one pair of opposite sides are equal and parallel,
Answer: Parallelogram

Question 2. Name the quadrilateral formed by joining the mid-points of the sides of a quadrilateral in order,
Answer: Parallelogram

Question 3. If $ABCD$ is a rectangle, then name the quadrilateral formed by joining the mid-points of its sides in:
Answer: Rhombus (But, if $ABCD$ is a square, then the name of the quadrilateral formed by joining the mid-points of its sides is also a square.)

Question 4. What do you mean by rhombus?
Answer: A rhombus is a parallelogram with four equal sides and opposite equal angles.

Question 5. Define parallelogram?
Answer: A parallelogram is a two-dimensional geometrical shape, whose sides are parallel to each other.

Question6. What do you mean by a quadrilateral?
Answer: A quadrilateral is a plane closed figure bounded by four-line segments.

Question 7. How many types of a parallelogram?
Answer: The three different types of a parallelogram are:
Square, Rectangle, Rhombus.

Question 8. Name the parallelogram if the diagonals of a parallelogram are perpendicular to each other.
Answer: Rhombus.

MULTIPLE CHOICE QUESTION

Question 1.
The ratio of the line segment joining the mid-points of any two sides of a triangle and the third side is given by
(a) $2:1$
(b) $1:2$
(c) $1:1$
(d) $2:3$

Question 2.
In a quadrilateral ABCD, equal diagonals AC and BD intersect at P, such that $AP = PC, BP = PD$ and $\angle BPC = 90°$. The quadrilateral is exactly
(a) A parallelogram
(b) A square
(c) A rhombus
(d) A rectangle

Question 3.
Diagonals of a parallelogram ABCD intersect at O. If ∠BOC = 90° and ∠BDC = 50°, the ∠OAB is
(a) 90°
(b) 50°
(c) 40°
(d) 10°

Question 4.
The triangle formed by joining the mid-points of the sides of an equilateral triangle is:
(a) An equilateral triangle
(b) An isosceles triangle
(c) A right-angled triangle
(d) None of these

Question 5.
The diagonals of a rectangle ABCD intersect each other at O. If ∠BOC = 44°, then ∠OAD =
(a) 58°
(b) 68°
(c) 64°
(d) 62°

Question 6.
If bisectors of ∠A and ∠B of a quadrilateral ABCD intersect each other at P, that of ∠B and ∠C at Q, that of ∠C and that ∠D at R and of ∠D and ∠A at S, then PQRS is a
(a) Rectangle
(b) Rhombus
(c) Parallelogram
(d) quadrilateral whose opposite angles are supplementary

Question 7.
The triangle formed by joining the mid-points of the sides of a right triangle is:
(a) A right triangle.
(b) An obtuse-angled triangle.
(c) An isosceles triangle.
(d) None of these.

Question 8.
The diagonals AC and BD of a parallelogram ABCD intersect each other at the point O. If ∠DAC = 32° and ∠AOB = 70°, then ∠DBC is equal to
(a) 24°
(b) 86°
(c) 38°
(d) 32°

Question 9.
In a square, diagonals are:
(a) Equal
(b) Not equal
(c) Half of each other
(d) None of these

Question 10.
In △ PQR, if S is the mid-point of PR, T lies on QR and ST = PQ then:
(a) $ST = \frac{1}{3}PQ$
(b) $ST = \frac{1}{2}PQ$
(c) $ST = PQ$
(d) None of these

ANSWER KEY

1.(b)	2.(a)	3.(a)	4.(a)	5.(d)	6.(c)	7.(a)	8.(b)	9.(a)	10.(b)

OBJECTIVE
To verify that in a triangle, the line joining the mid-points of any two sides is parallel to the third side and half of it by paper folding and pasting.

MATERIAL REQUIRED
Glazed papers, a pair of scissors, pencil, eraser, glue stick, white sheet.

THEORY
1. Concept of angles, triangles and mid-points.
2. **Concept of corresponding angles:** If a transversal cuts two straight lines such that their corresponding angles are equal, then the lines are parallel.

PROCEDURE
1. Draw ΔABC on the yellow glazed paper of any measurement and paste it is on a white sheet.
2. Find mid-points of the two sides (say AB and AC) of a triangle by paper folding. We obtain D and E as mid-points of AB and AC respectively in the 1st triangle.

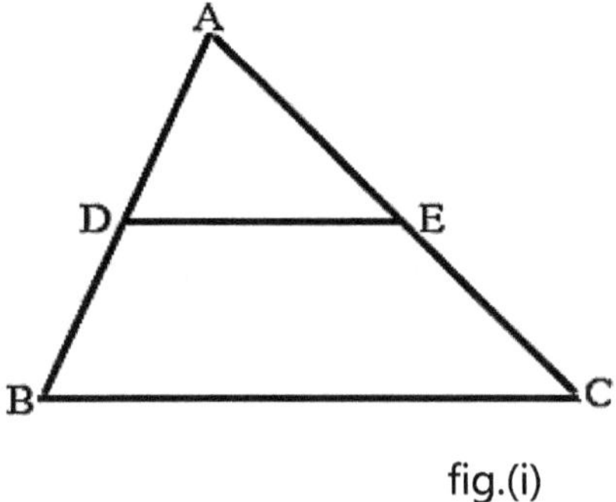

fig.(i)

3. Draw horizontal line DE. Similarly, find the mid-point of side BC and name it F as shown in fig. (ii).

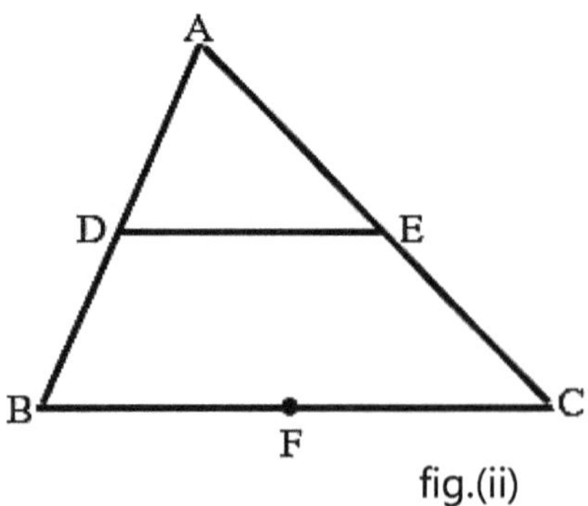

fig.(ii)

4. Trace the ΔABC on tracing paper and cut ΔABC along line DE as shown in fig.(iii).

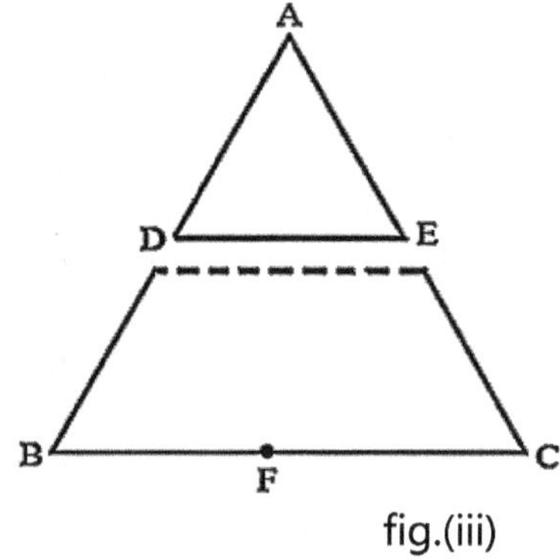

fig.(iii)

5. Paste this cut out of triangle ADE [fig. (iii)] on ΔABC of fig. (ii) such that AE coincides with EC and ED lies on CB and point D coincides with F as shown in fig. (iv).

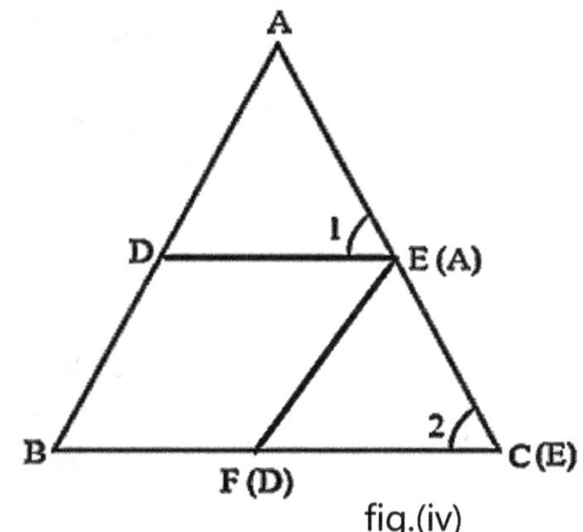

fig.(iv)

6. ΔADE completely covers ΔEFC.

OBSERVATION

We observe that ΔADE exactly overlaps ΔEFC.

∴ $\angle 1 = \angle 2$ (corresponding angles)

AC is any transversal line intersecting the lines DE and BC.

∴ DE ∥ BC.

By paper folding, we observe that, in fig (iv) F, the mid-point of BC coincides with D.

DE = FC (As DE superimposes on FC)

Or $DE = FC = \dfrac{BC}{2}$

RESULT

Hence, it is verified that the line joining the mid-points of two sides of a triangle is parallel to the third side and half of it.

LEARNING OUTCOME

Line segment joining the mid-points of any two sides of a triangle is parallel to the third side and is equal to half of it. This is true for all types of triangles like an acute-angled triangle, obtuse-angled triangle and right-angled triangle.

Students can verify this theorem in different triangles, e.g., obtuse-angled triangle, right-angled triangle, equilateral triangles, scalene triangles.

VIVA-VOCE

Question 1. State the mid-point theorem.
Answer: The line drawn through the mid-point of one side of a triangle and parallel to another side of the triangle, bisects the third side of the triangle.

Question 2. What is the area of a triangle?
Answer: Area of triangle $= \frac{1}{2} \times$ base $\times$ height

Question 3. Name the different triangles based on their sides.
Answer: Equilateral triangle, scalene triangle, isosceles triangle.

Question 4. In a triangle, the line drawn through the mid-point of one side is parallel to another side, what is the ratio of the parallel line to the third side?
Answer: $1:2$.

Question 5. Is the mid-point theorem applicable in any type of triangle?
Answer: Yes.

Question 6. In a triangle, the line is drawn through the mid-points of two sides, then what will be the relation between the line and the third side?
Answer: The line will be parallel to the third side.

Question 7. In $\triangle ABC$, D, E, F are the mid-points of the sides BC, CA, and AB respectively, and $\angle BAC = 70°$, what is the value of $\angle EDF$?
Answer: $70°$

Question 8. Name the different triangles based on their angles.
Answer: Acute angled triangle, obtuse-angled triangle and right-angled triangle.

MULTIPLE CHOICE QUESTION

Question 1.
What is the length of DE if DE ∥ BC, $BC = 18$ cm and D and E are mid-points of AB and AC?

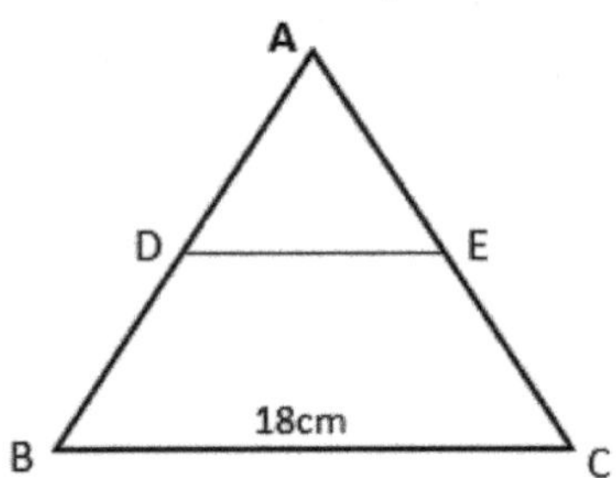

(a) 18 cm
(b) 15 cm
(c) 9 cm
(d) 20 cm

Question 2.
If $ABCR$ and $PQRS$ are rectangles and B is the mid-point of PR, find the ratio of $\frac{AC}{PR}$?

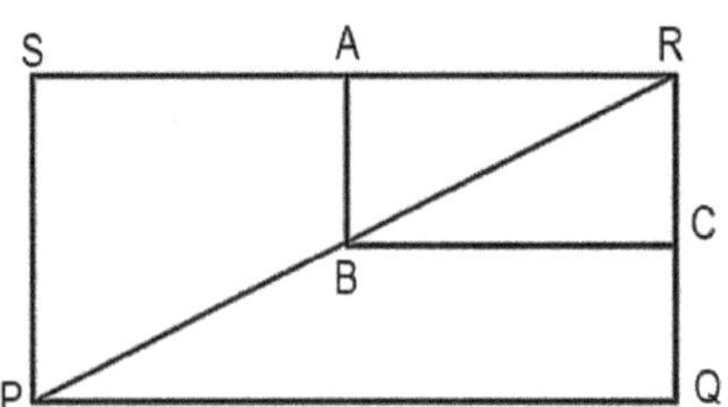

(a) $\frac{1}{2}$
(b) 2
(c) 1
(d) $\frac{5}{2}$

Question 3.

Find the ratio of the angles $\angle D : \angle E : \angle F$ of $\triangle$ DEF formed by joining the mid-points of the sides of $\triangle$ ABC.

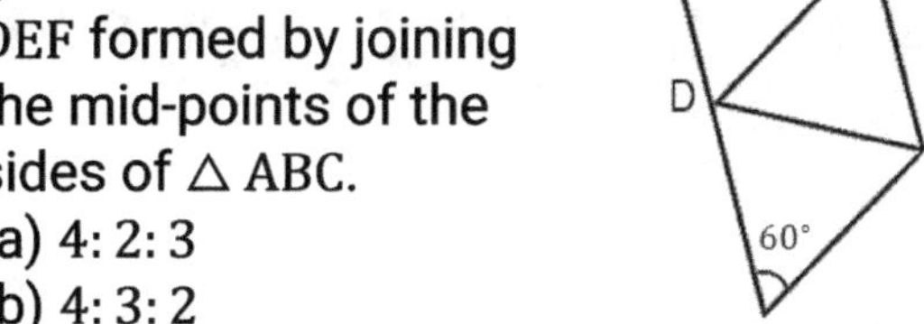

(a) $4:2:3$
(b) $4:3:2$
(c) $2:3:5$
(d) $5:3:2$

Question 4.

Find the perimeter of $\triangle ABC$, if the perimeter of $\triangle$ PQR is 36 cm and A, B and C are mid-points.

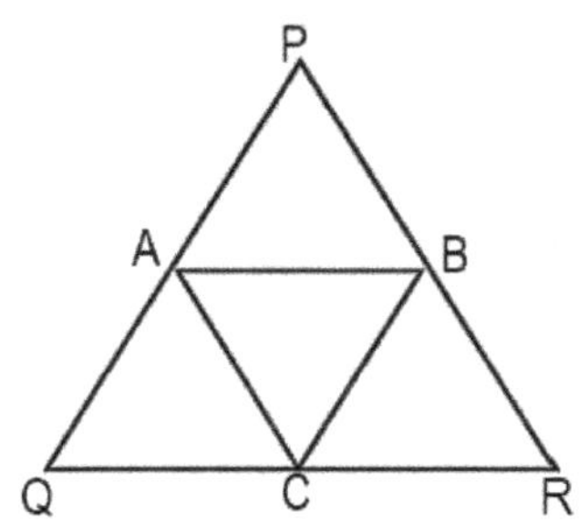

(a) 9 cm
(b) 18 cm
(c) 20 cm
(d) 36 cm

Question 5.

Find the ratio of $\frac{(AB + CD)}{EG}$ if EG || AB and AB || DC and E and G are the mid-points.

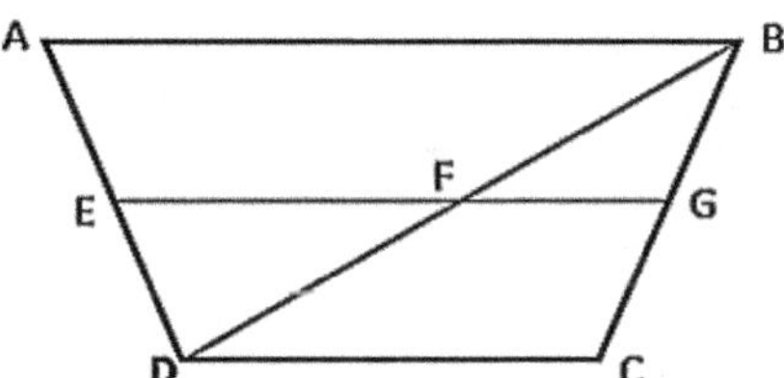

(a) 1
(b) $\frac{1}{2}$
(c) 2
(d) $\frac{3}{2}$

Question 6.

What is the ratio of $\frac{AC}{CF}$ if AD and BE are the median and DF || BE?

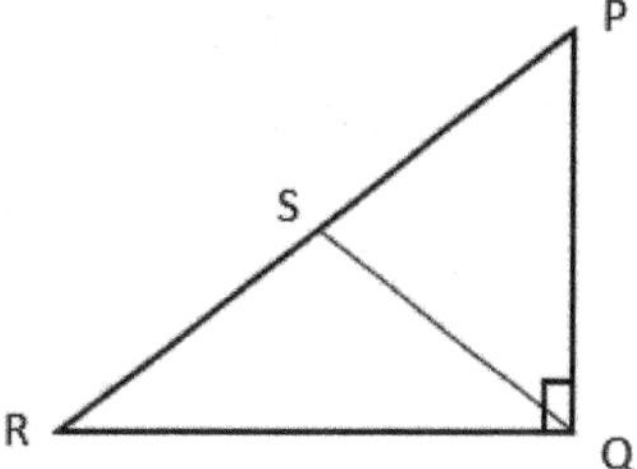

(a) 4
(b) 1
(c) $\frac{1}{4}$
(d) $\frac{1}{2}$

Question 7.

Which of the following relation is correct if S is the mid-point of PR?

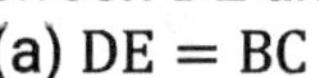

(a) $QS = PR$
(b) $QS = \frac{1}{2PR}$
(c) $QS = 2PR$
(d) $QS = \frac{1}{4PR}$

Question 8.

From the diagram below, if D and E are mid-points of the lines AB and AC respectively and if DE || BC, then what is the relation between DE and BC?

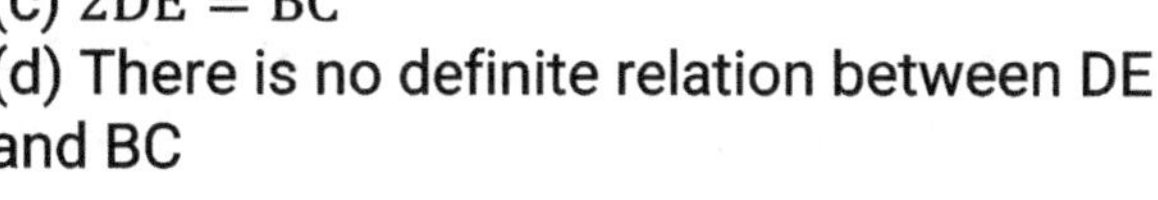

(a) $DE = BC$
(b) $3DE = BC$
(c) $2DE = BC$
(d) There is no definite relation between DE and BC

OBJECTIVE
To explore the similarities and differences between the different quadrilaterals like a parallelogram, rectangle, rhombus, and square with respect to their diagonals.

MATERIAL REQUIRED
Glazed papers, ruler, a pair of scissors, pencil, tracing paper.

THEORY
Properties of parallelogram, rectangle, square, rhombus.
1. In parallelogram, diagonals are not equal.
2. In a rectangle, diagonals are equal.
3. In a rhombus, diagonals are not equal but bisect each other at 90°
4. In a square, diagonals are equal and bisect each other at 90°.

PROCEDURE
CASE I:
1. Make a parallelogram on a glazed paper by paper folding and name it ABCD. Join AC and BD.
2. Draw and cut replicas of ΔABC and ΔBCD. Coincide the diagonals AC and BD.

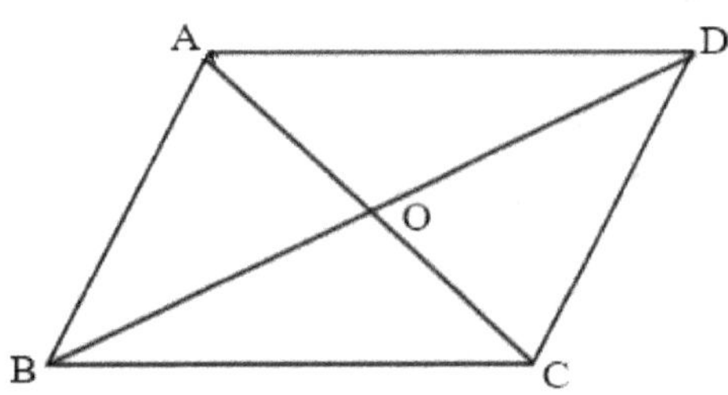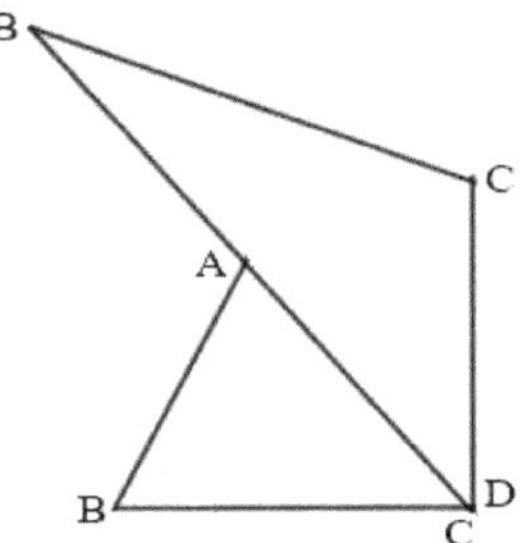

OBSERVATION:
We observe that diagonal AC ≠ diagonal BD.

CASE II
1. Make a rectangle by paper folding on glazed paper. Name it as PQRS. Join PR and QS.
2. Cut replicas of ΔPQS and ΔPQR and name them ΔBCA and ΔEFD.

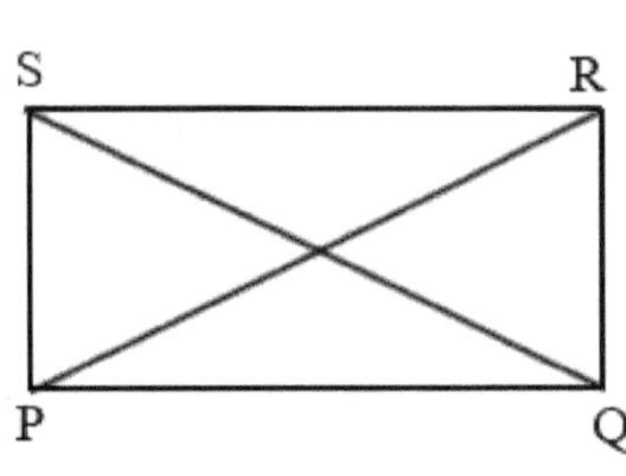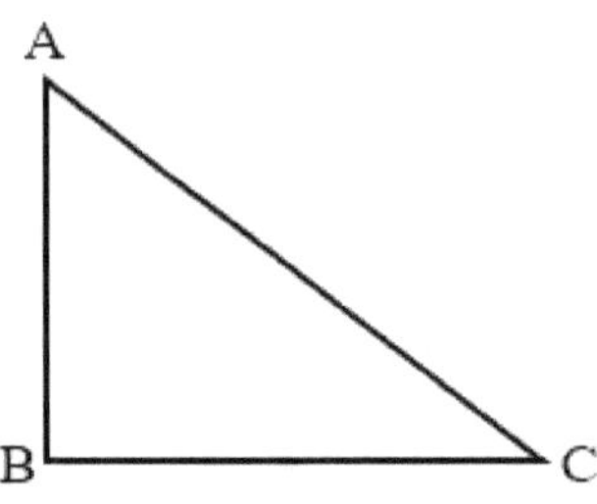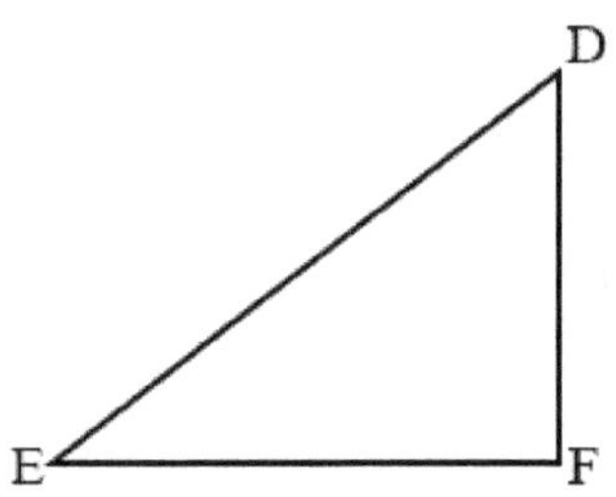

3. Place two replicas such that AC and ED concise each other and side AB is opposite to side FD.

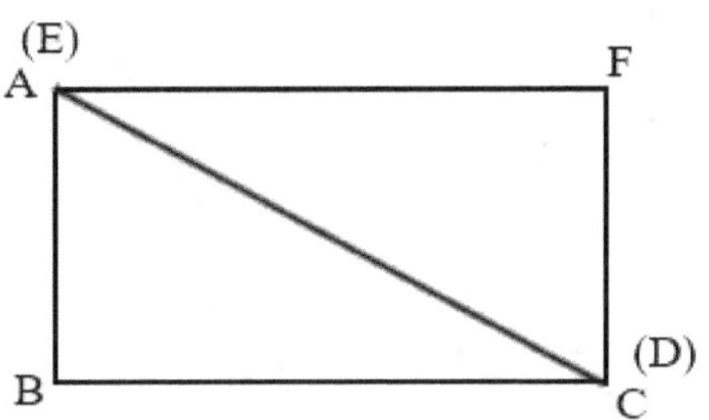

OBSERVATION:
>   Here we notice that AC = DE. (As they overlap each other)
> $\therefore$ diagonal AC = diagonal DE
> $\therefore$ QS = PR

CASE III:

1. Make a rhombus by paper folding on glazed paper. Name it as ABCD.Join AC and BD.
2. Draw and cut replicas of $\triangle ABC$ and $\triangle DCB$ and name them as $\triangle PQR$ and $\triangle MNO'$ respectively.
3. Place two replicas such that PR and MO' coincide each other.

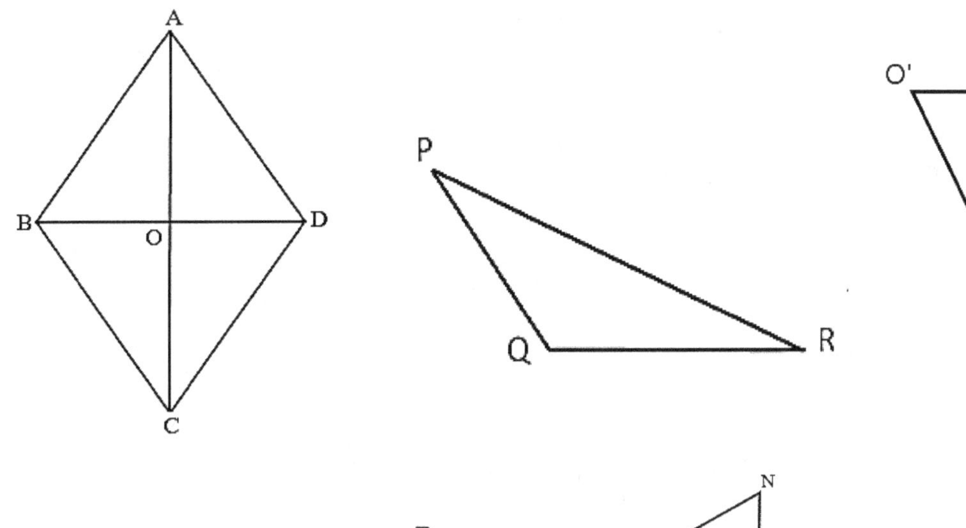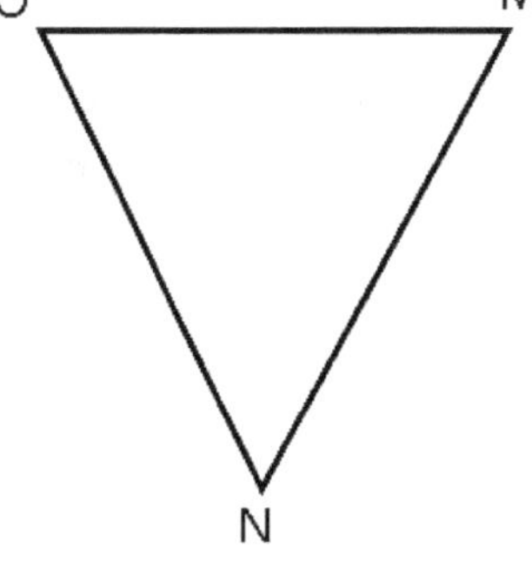

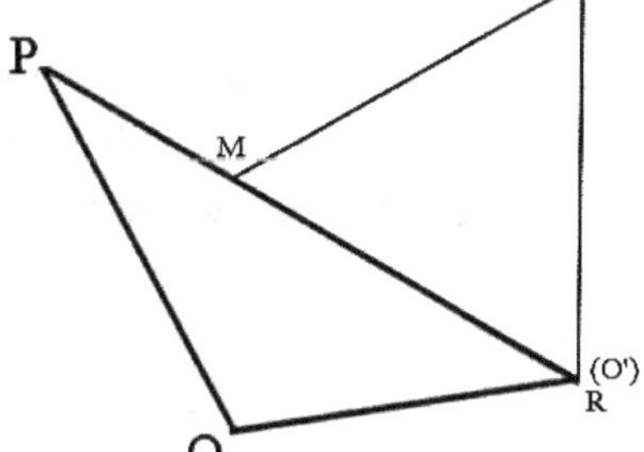

OBSERVATION:
>   We observe that   PR $\neq$ O'M.
> $\therefore$ diagonal AC $\neq$ diagonal BD

4. Draw and cut replicas of $\triangle AOB$ and $\triangle BOC$ and verify the congruency of two triangles by placing one over the other.

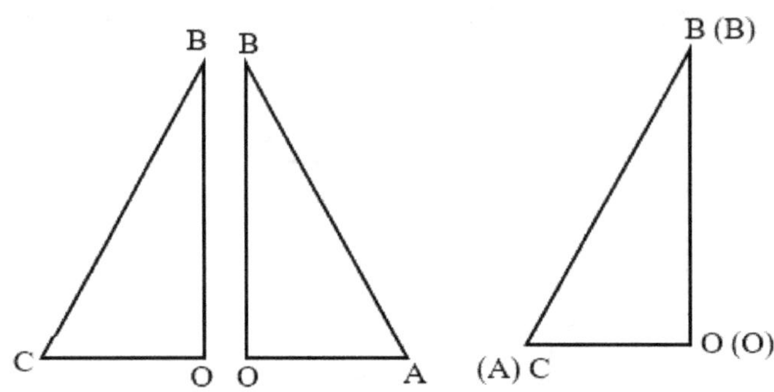

Here

$$BC = AB$$
$$OB = BO$$
$$OC = OA$$

$$\therefore \qquad \triangle BOC = \triangle BOA$$
$$\therefore \qquad \angle BOC = \angle BOA$$
$$\therefore \qquad \angle BOC + \angle BOA = 180° \qquad \text{............ (linear pair angles)}$$
$$2\angle BOC = 180° \qquad \text{....... from (i)}$$
$$\therefore \qquad \angle BOC = 90°$$

Thus, it is verified that in a rhombus, diagonals are not equal but bisect each other at 90°.

CASE IV:

1. Make a square by paper folding on glazed paper. Name it as PQRS. Join PR and SQ.
2. Draw and cut replicas of ΔPQS and ΔPQR.

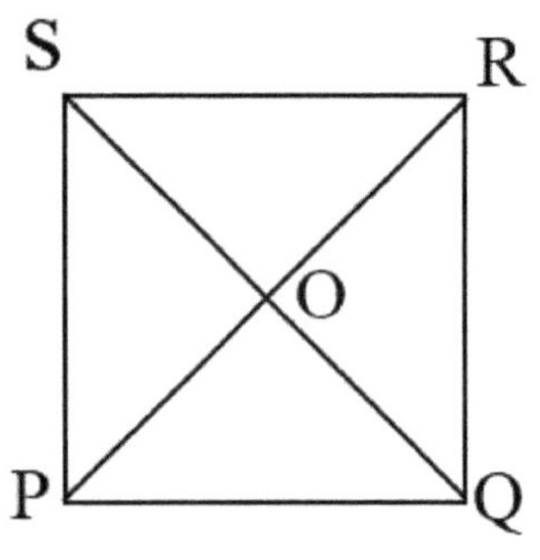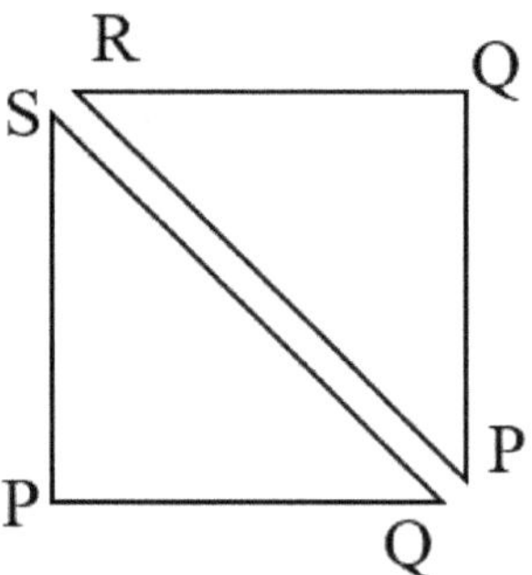

3. Place two replicas along their diagonals SQ and PR. Here, we observe that both diagonals overlap each other completely. Thus, diagonal SQ = diagonal PR.
4. Draw and cut replicas of ΔPOQ and ΔPOS. Place these replicas as shown in fig. below.

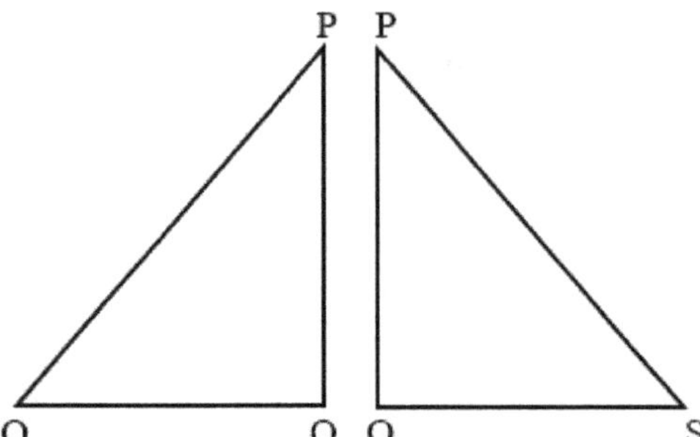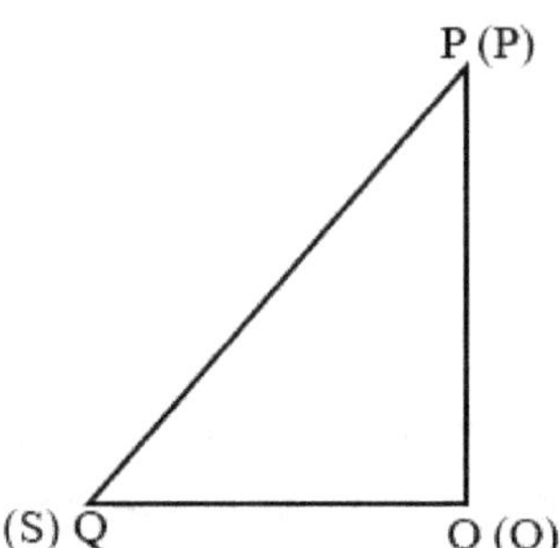

OBSERVATION:

Here,

$$PQ = SP \qquad \text{(sides of a square)}$$
$$OP = OP \qquad \text{(common side)}$$
$$OQ = OS \qquad \text{(By observation)}$$
$$\triangle POQ = \triangle POS \qquad \text{(By SSS)}$$
$$\therefore \qquad \angle POQ = \angle POS \qquad \text{(C.P.C.T.)}$$
$$\text{But } \angle POQ + \angle POS = 180° \qquad \text{(linear pair angles)}$$
$$2\angle POQ = 180°$$
$$\angle POQ = 90°$$

This implies that in a square, diagonals are equal and bisect each other at 90°.

OBSERVATION

By paper folding and cutting activity, it is very much clear that rectangle,square, rhombus, and parallelogram differ by their diagonal properties.

In a parallelogram, diagonals are not equal, in rectangle diagonals are equal, in rhombus diagonals are not equal but bisect each other at 90°, in a square, diagonals are equal and bisect each other at 90°.

RESULT

We verified that, in a parallelogram, diagonals are not equal, in square diagonals are equal and bisect each other at 90°. In a rectangle, diagonals are equal and bisect each other at 90°.In a rhombus, diagonals are not equal but bisect at 90°.In this way, these figures differentiate each other based on their diagonals.

LEARNING OUTCOME

Though square, rectangle, and rhombus all have the properties of a parallelogram but they are different based on their diagonals.

ACTIVITY TIME

Draw all types of quadrilaterals on the same plane by using different glazedpaper.

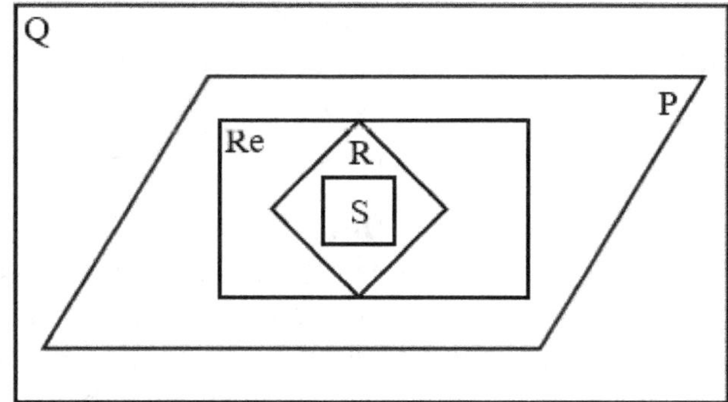

Q – Quadrilateral
P – Parallelogram
Re – Rectangle
R – Rhombus
S – Square

We conclude that all squares are rhombus, rectangle and parallelogram.

Question 1. What is the angle sum property of a quadrilateral?
Answer: The sum of all angles of a quadrilateral is a complete angle, i.e. 360°.

Question 2. The sum of three angles of a quadrilateral is 280°. Find the measure of the fourth angle.
Answer: Fourth angle = 360° − 280° = 80°

Question 3. Is it true that every parallelogram is a rectangle?
Answer: No, only that parallelogram is a rectangle whose all angles are 90°.

Question 4. In which quadrilateral(s), diagonals are perpendicular to each other?
Answer: Rhombus

Question 5. Is it true that the diagonals of a rhombus are equal?
Answer: No

Question 6. What are the conditions that any quadrilateral be a square?
Answer: (i) All four sides of a quadrilateral are equal.
(ii) Each angle of a quadrilateral is 90°.
(iii) Diagonals are equal and bisect each other.

Question 7. Is it true that a parallelogram is always a trapezium, but a trapezium is not always a parallelogram?
Answer: True

Question 8. How many vertices a quadrilateral has?
Answer: A quadrilateral has 4 vertices.

Question 9. Can all the angles of a quadrilateral be right angles? Give reason.
Answer: Yes, all the angles of a quadrilateral can be right angles. e.g., Square and rectangle.

MULTIPLE CHOICE QUESTION

Question 1.
Which of the following is not true for a parallelogram?
(a) Diagonals bisect each other
(b) Opposite sides are equal
(c) Opposite angles are equal
(d) Opposite angles are bisected by the diagonals

Question 2.
A quadrilateral with only one pair of opposite sides parallel is called:
(a) Trapezium
(b) Square
(c) Rectangle
(d) Rhombus

Question 3.
The consecutive angles of a parallelogram are:
(a) Complementary
(b) Supplementary
(c) Equal
(d) None of these

Question 4.
The quadrilateral formed by joining the mid-points of the sides of a quadrilateral ABCD taken in order is a square only if:
(a) ABCD is a rhombus
(b) Diagonals of ABCD are equal
(c) Diagonals of ABCD are equal and perpendicular
(d) Diagonals of ABCD are perpendicular

<table>
<tr><td>

Question 5.
If in a parallelogram its diagonals bisect each other at right angles and are equal, then it is a
(a) Square
(b) Rhombus
(c) Rectangle
(d) Parallelogram

Question 6.
Which of the following quadrilaterals has two pairs of adjacent sides equal and diagonals intersecting at right angles?
(a) Square.
(b) Rhombus.
(c) Kite.
(d) Rectangle.

</td><td>

Question 7.
Which of the following is not true?
(a) Every square is a rectangle
(b) Every rectangle is a quadrilateral
(c) Every parallelogram is a trapezium
(d) None of these

Question 8.
If in a parallelogram its diagonals bisect each other and are equal then it is a,
(a) Squares
(b) Rectangle
(c) Rhombus
(d) Parallelogram

</td></tr>
</table>

ANSWER KEY

1. (d)	2. (a)	3. (b)	4. (c)	5. (a)	6. (b)	7. (c)	8. (b)

AREA OF A PARALLELOGRAM

OBJECTIVE

To show that the area of a parallelogram is equal to the product of its base and corresponding height by using paper cutting and pasting.

MATERIAL REQUIRED

Glazed papers, pencil, a pair of scissors, glue stick.

THEORY

1. Construction of parallelogram by paper folding.
2. Area of rectangle = length × breadth
3. Area of parallelogram = base × corresponding height.

PROCEDURE

1. Draw a parallelogram by paper folding using coloured glazed paper and name it ABCD.
2. Cut the parallelogram with the help of scissors.
3. In the parallelogram, draw a perpendicular from a vertex D to its opposite side AB of the parallelogram ABCD by paper folding.
4. We will get a crease along with DE. Dark the colour in ΔADE [fig (i)]. Now cut it along DE. We will get two pieces, one triangle named as AED and the other one a trapezium named E'D'CB as shown in fig.(ii).

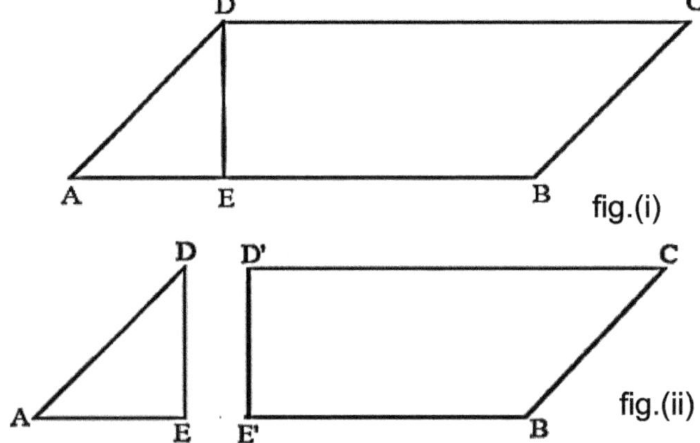

5. Paste this triangular piece AED on the other side of trapezium such that its side AD coincides with BC [fig.(iii)].

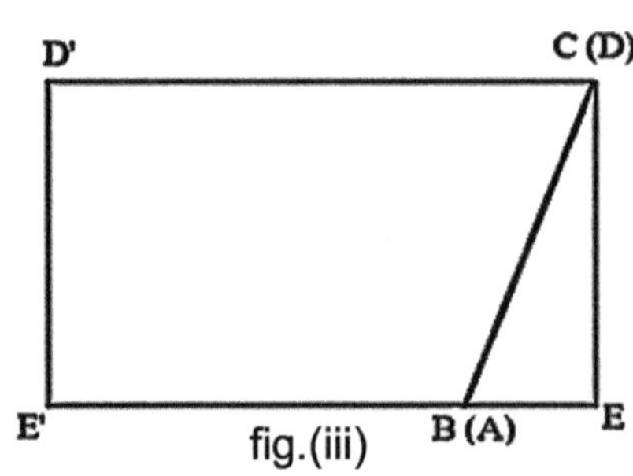

6. After pasting, we get a rectangle E'ECD' with length as $E'B + BE = E'E = D'C = AB$ and breadth as $E'D' = EC$.

OBSERVATION

We observe that new figure D'E'EC is a rectangle.

$$\text{Area of parallelogram ABCD} = \text{Area of rectangle E'ECD'}$$
$$= \text{length} \times \text{breadth}$$
$$= E'E \times D'E'$$
$$= AB \times DE$$

Hence, Area of parallelogram $\quad = \text{Base} \times \text{Height}$

RESULT

It is verified that the area of a parallelogram is equal to the product of its base and corresponding height by the paper cutting and pasting method.

LEARNING OUTCOME

We can draw a perpendicular from different vertices on opposite sides of a parallelogram and verify that the area of the parallelogram is the product of base and height.

Area of a parallelogram with the same base and the same height are identical. This leads to a famous theorem:

"Parallelogram between the same parallel lines and on the same base are equal in area."

ACTIVITY TIME

Verify the area of a parallelogram is equal to the product of its base and corresponding height in which perpendicular falls outside the base of the parallelogram.

VIVA-VOCE

Question 1. How does a diagonal of a parallelogram form two triangles of equal area?
Answer: A diagonal of a parallelogram divides it into two triangles of equal area.

Question 2. In a parallelogram if $AB = 4$ cm, $BC = 6$ cm, $CD = 8$ cm and $AD = 10$ cm then find perimeter of paralllelogram.
Answer: $P = 28$ cm.

Question 3. If one side of a parallelogram is 10 cm and its area is 60 cm². Find the corresponding altitude.
Answer: Side of the parallelogram (base) = 10 cm
Area of the parallelogram = 60 cm²
Now, base × altitude = 60 cm²
$$\Rightarrow \text{altitude} = \frac{60 \text{ cm}^2}{10 \text{ cm}} = 6 \text{ cm}$$

Question 4. If the base of a parallelogram is 5 cm and the corresponding altitude is 3 cm. Find the area of the parallelogram.
Answer: Base of the parallelogram = 5 cm
Corresponding altitude of the parallelogram = 3 cm
Area of the parallelogram = 5×3 cm² = 15 cm².

Question 5. What is the area of a triangle?
Answer: Area of a triangle $= \frac{1}{2} \times$ base $\times$ height.

Question 6. Define an altitude of a quadrilateral.
Answer: An altitude of a quadrilateral is a perpendicular line segment joining a vertex of the quadrilateral to the opposite side

Question 1.
In the figure, ABC and BDE are two equilateral triangles such that D is the mid-point of BC. If AB intersects BC in F, then we have

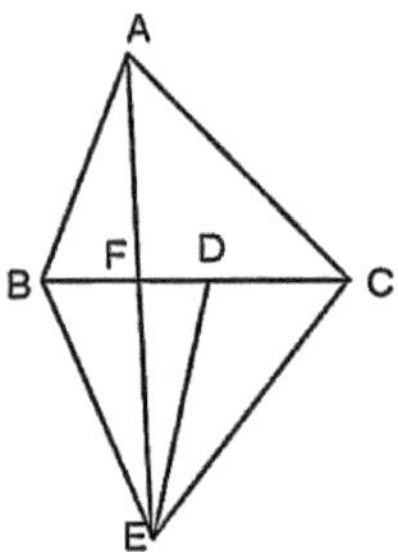

(a) Area $(\triangle BDE) = \dfrac{1}{4}$ area $(\triangle ABC)$

(b) Area $(\triangle BDE) = \dfrac{1}{2}$ area $(\triangle BAF)$

(c) Area $(\triangle BEF) = 2$ area $(\triangle FED)$

(d) Area $(\triangle FED) = \dfrac{1}{4}$ area $(\triangle AFC)$

Question 2.
If Diagonals AC and BD of a quadrilateral ABCD intersect at O in such a way that $ar(\triangle AOD) = ar(\triangle BOC)$. Then ABCD is a:
(i) Parallelogram
(ii) Rectangle
(iii) Square
(iv) Trapezium

Question 3.
The median of a triangle divides it into two
(a) Triangles of equal area
(b) Congruent triangles
(c) Right triangles
(d) Isosceles triangles

Question 4.
Is a rhombus a parallelogram?
(a) Yes
(b) No
(c) Can't say
(d) None of these

Question 5.
In the given figure, if ar($\triangle$ACL) = ar ($\triangle$ADM), then
(a) CO = OD
(b) AC = AB
(c) CO > OD
(d) CO < OD

Question 6.
If ar(parallelogram ABCD) = 25 cm^2 and ar ($\triangle$ BCD) = x cm^2, then the value of x is

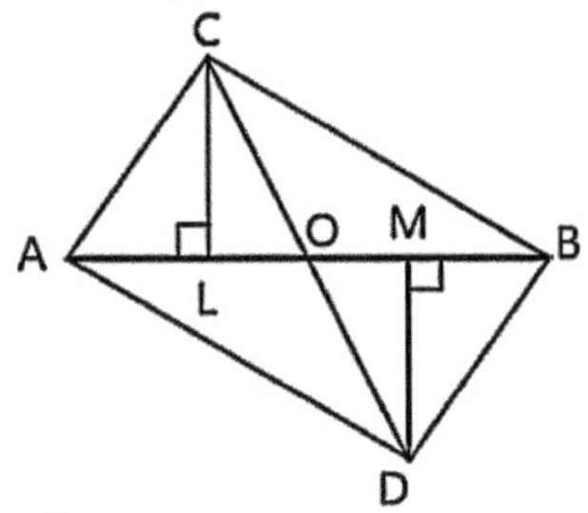

(a) 25 cm^2
(b) 50 cm^2
(c) 12.5 cm
(d) 12.5 cm^2

Question 7.
Given, a triangle ABC and E is the mid-point of median AD of $\triangle ABC$. If $ar(\triangle BED) = 20$ cm^2, then $ar(\triangle ABC)$ is
(a) 10 cm^2
(b) 5 cm^2
(c) 60 cm^2
(d) 80 cm^2

Question 8.
Measure of one angle of a parallelogram is 2/3 of its measure of the adjacent angle. Measure of the smaller angle of the parallelogram is:
(a) 54°
(b) 72°
(c) 81°
(d) 108°

ANSWER KEY

1.(a)	2.(d)	3.(a)	4.(a)	5.(a)	6.(a)	7.(c)	8.(b)

ACTIVITY 21

AREA OF PARALLELOGRAMS ON THE SAME BASE AND BETWEEN THE SAME PARALLELS

OBJECTIVE
To show that the parallelograms on the same base and between the same parallel lines are equal in the area by paper cutting and pasting.

MATERIAL REQUIRED
Glazed paper, a pair of scissors, glue stick, geometry box.

THEORY
1. Area of parallelogram = base × height
2. The shortest distance between two parallel lines is the perpendicular distance between parallel lines and it remains same for that pair of parallel lines.

PROCEDURE
1. Draw a parallelogram by paper folding activity.
2. Cut this parallelogram using scissors and name it as ABCD, [fig.(i)].

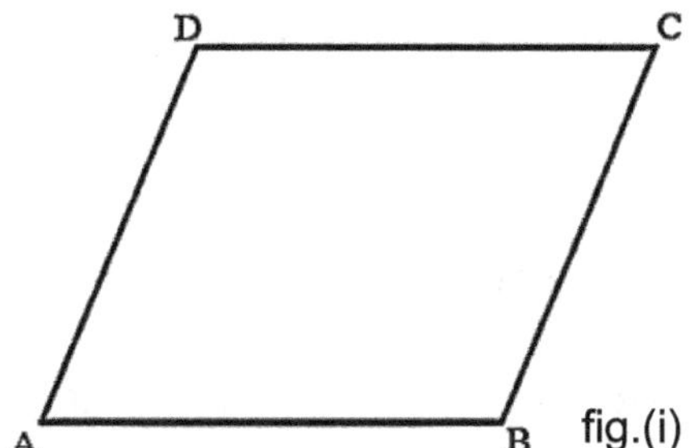

fig.(i)

3. Mark any point E on DC.
4. From A fold the parallelogram till the point E (any point on DC). A crease AE is formed, fill another colour in △ADE. [fig. (ii)].

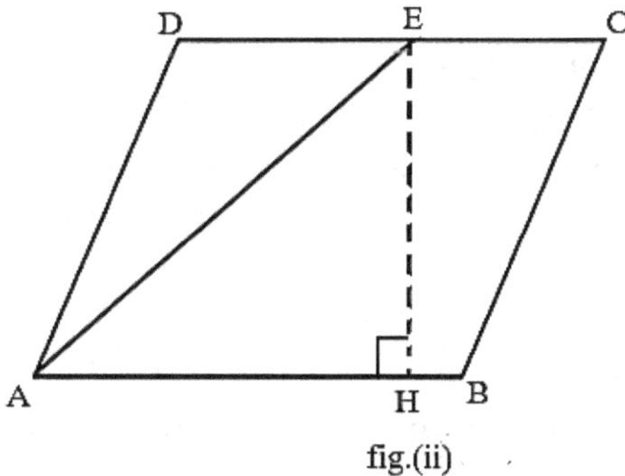

fig.(ii)

5. Cut the parallelogram ABCD along AE to get △AED.
6. Paste the △AED on the other side along BC of parallelogram ABCD as shown in fig.(iii).

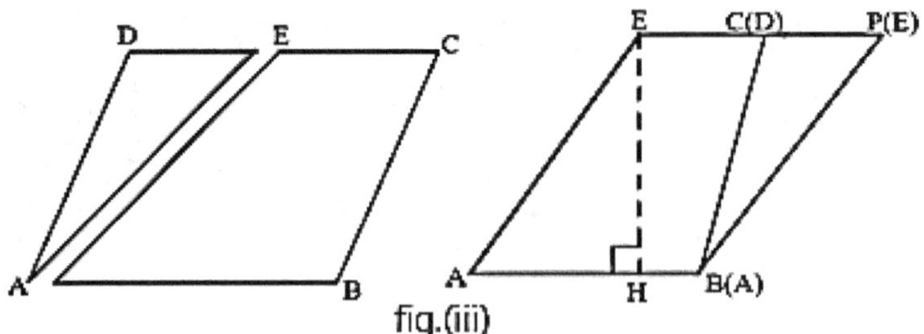

7. We get a new parallelogram AEPB.

OBSERVATION

1. We observe that the two parallelograms ABCD and ABPE have same base AB.
2. Two parallelograms lie between same parallel lines, i.e., AB and CD and the height between them are same at all points.

   By formula, area of parallelogram= base × height

   $$\text{ar } (\parallel \text{gm ABCD}) = AB \times EH$$
   $$\text{ar } (\parallel \text{gm ABPE}) = AB \times EH$$

RESULT

We have verified that two parallelograms lying on same base and between same parallel lines are equal in area.

LEARNING OUTCOME

Students follow that the parallelograms on the same base and between the same parallels have same area.

ACTIVITY TIME

1. This theorem can be proved by using graph paper. Students will try this and verify the theorem.
2. Prove that areas of a rectangle and a square of same height and on the same base are equal by using the paper cutting and pasting method.

VIVA-VOCE

Question 1. What is the relationship between the areas of the parallelograms on the same base (or equal bases) and between the same parallel lines?
Answer: Both areas are same.

Question 2. Do the diagonals of a parallelogram divide it into two triangles of the equal base?
Answer: No, the diagonals of a parallelogram divide it into four triangles of an equal base.

Question 3. What is the altitude of a parallelogram?
Answer: Altitude of a parallelogram is the perpendicular distance between two parallel sides.

Question 4. How would you define the area of a parallelogram?
Answer: Area of a parallelogram is the product of its base and the corresponding altitude.

Question 5. What are the types of parallelograms?

Answer: Parallelograms are of three types, i.e., rectangle, square and rhombus.

Question 6. Find the perimeter of the following parallelogram:

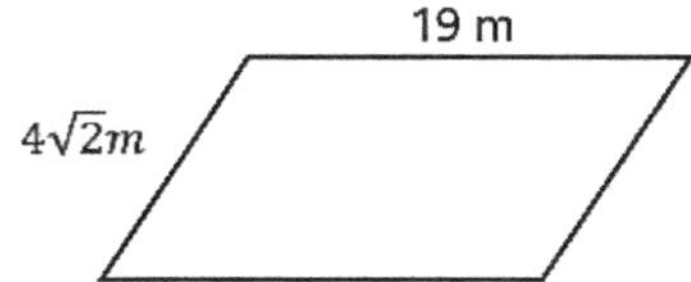

Answers: $38 + 8\sqrt{2}m$

Question 7. Is it correct that every square and rhombus are parallelograms?

Answer: Yes, because opposite sides of these figures are parallel and equal.

Question 8. Adjacent sides of a rectangle are 16 cm and 8 cm. Find the area of the rectangle.

Answer: Area of rectanlge $= 16\text{ cm} \times 8\text{ cm}$
$$= 128 \text{ cm}$$

MULTIPLE CHOICE QUESTION

Question 1.
Find the area of parallelogram ABCD if AE: EB = 1: 2.

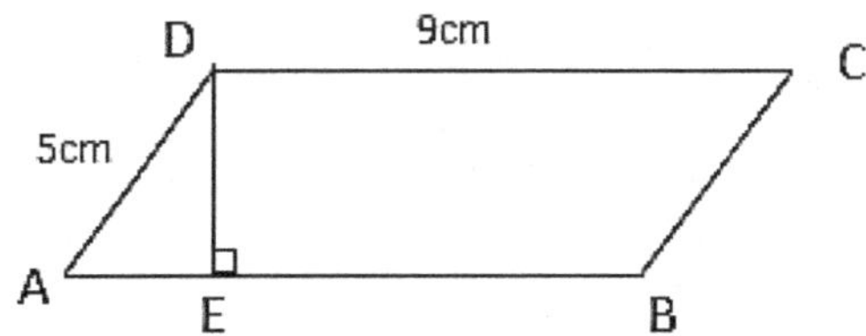

(a) 25 m²
(b) 22.5 m²
(c) 36 m²
(d) 45 m²

Question 2.
From the diagram given below, if area of triangle ABC is ar (ABD) and area of triangle ACD is ar (ACD), then what is the relation between ar (ABD) and ar (ACD)?

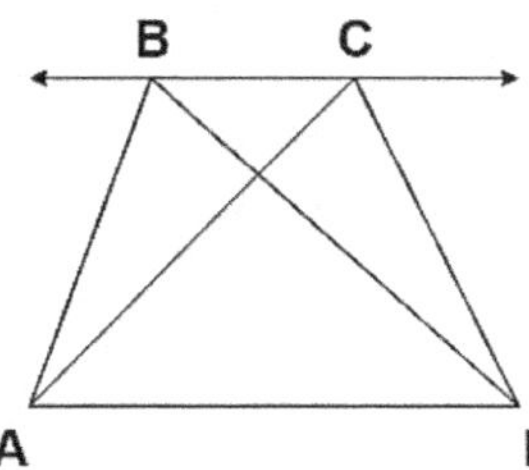

(a) ar (ABD) = 0.5ar(ACD)
(b) ar (ABC) = 4ar (ACD)
(c) ar (ABD) = 2ar (ACD)
(d) ar (ABD) = ar (ACD)

Question 3.
Find the ratio of the area of parallelogram ABCD to the area of parallelogram PQRS if A, B, C, and D are mid-points of a parallelogram.

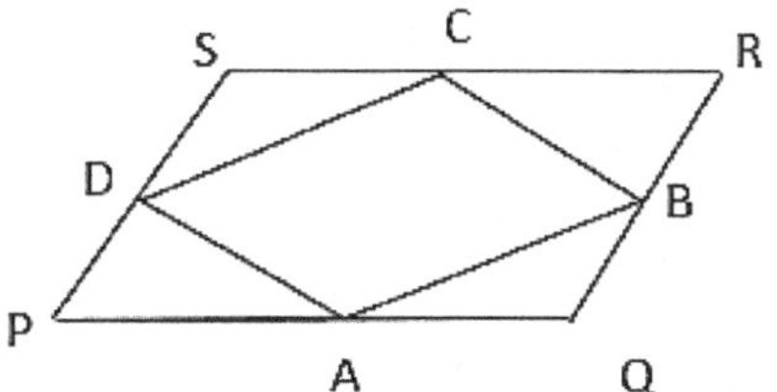

(a) $\frac{1}{2}$
(b) 1
(c) 2
(d) 3

Question 4.
Which of following relation is correct if ABCD is a parallelogram?

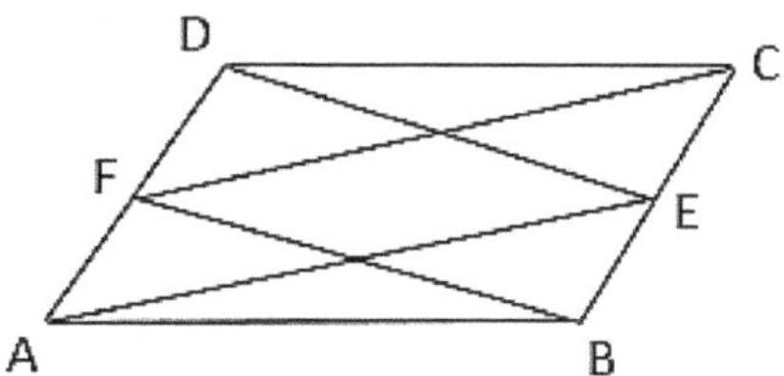

(a) ar (ADE) < ar (CDF)
(b) ar (ADE) > ar (CDF)
(c) ar (ADE) = ar (CDF)
(d) ar (ADE) = 1/2ar (CDF)

Question 5.
Find the ratio of the area of parallelogram AEFD to the area of parallelogram EBCF if E and F are mid-points of AB and CD respectively.

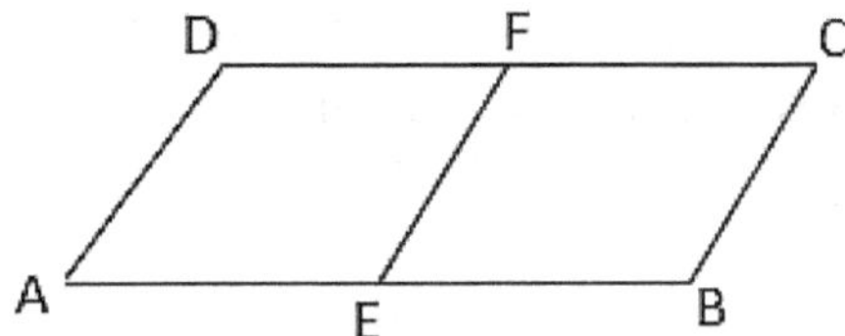

(a) 1
(b) 2
(c) 4
(d) 3

Question 6.
From the diagram given below, if area of parallelogram ABCD is ar (ABCD) and area of parallelogram AEFD is ar (AEFD), then what is the relation between ar(ABCD) and ar(AEFD)?
(a) ar$(ABCD)$ = ar$(AEFD)$
(b) ar$(ABCD)$ < ar$(AEFD)$
(c) ar$(ABCD)$ > ar$(AEFD)$
(d) There is no relation between areas of the two parallelograms

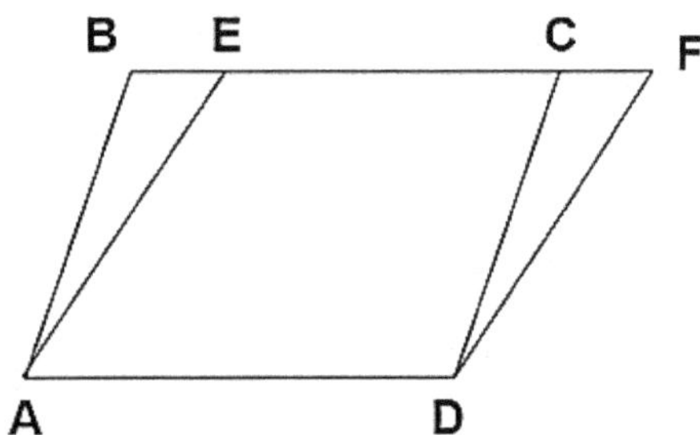

Question 7.
Find the area of parallelogram ABQR if area of parallelogram PQRS is 150 cm^2, A and B are mid-points of PQ and RS.

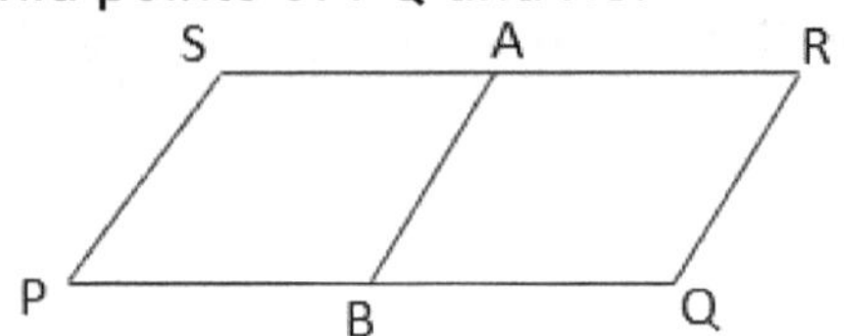

(a) 100 m^2
(b) 300 m^2
(c) 150 m^2
(d) 75 m^2

Question 8.
From the diagram given below, if area of parallelogram ABCD is ar (ABCD) and area of triangle AED is ar (AED), then what is the relation between ar (ABCD) and ar (AED)?
(a) ar (ABCD) = 0.5ar(AED)
(b) ar (ABCD) = 4ar(AED)
(c) ar (ABCD) = 2ar (AED)
(d) ar $(ABCD)$ = ar (AED)

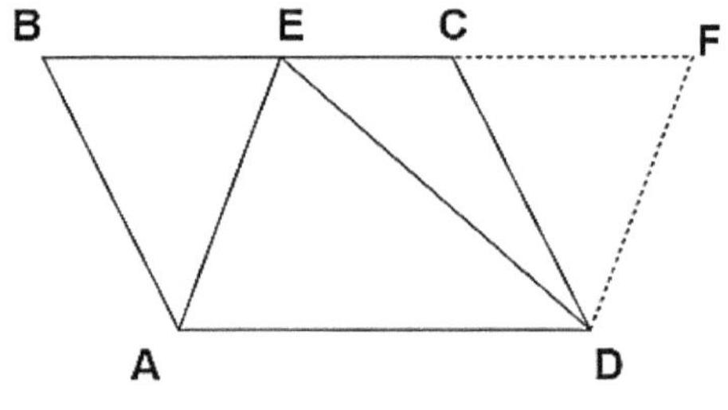

ANSWER KEY

1. (c)	2. (d)	3. (a)	4. (c)	5. (a)	6. (a)	7. (d)	8. (c)

OBJECTIVE

To show that the triangles on the same base and between the same parallel lines are equal in area experimentally.

MATERIAL REQUIRED

Glazed papers, a pair of scissors, a pencil, glue stick, white sheet.

THEORY

1. Familiarity with triangles.
2. Formula for the area of triangle $= \frac{1}{2} \times$ base $\times$ height
3. Shortest distance between the two parallel lines.

PROCEDURE

1. Draw any triangle on a glazed paper and name it ABC.
2. Cut the triangle and paste it on the white sheet as shown in fig.(i).

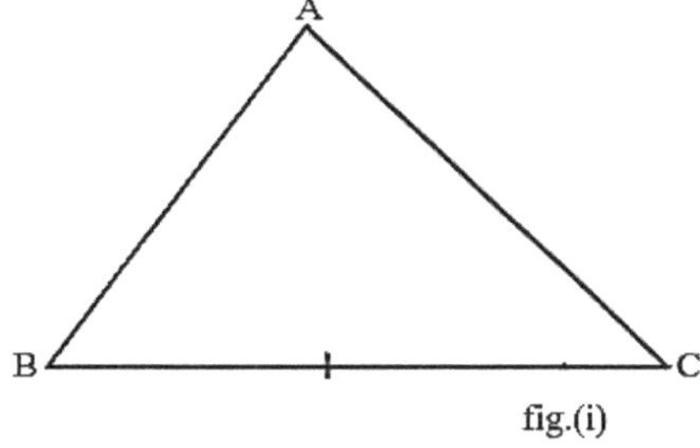

fig.(i)

3. Cut another triangle EGH such that $EH = BC$ [fig.(ii)]

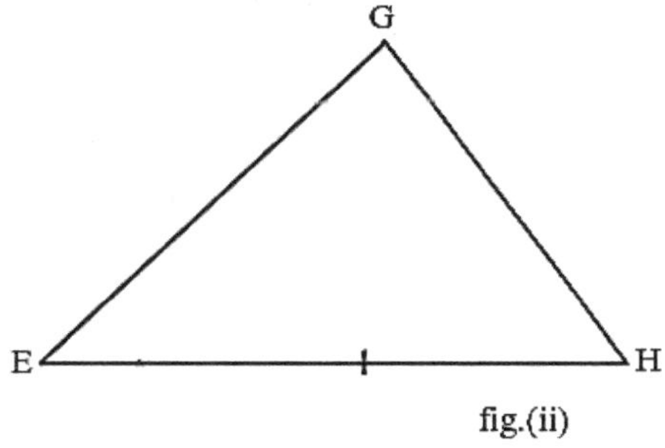

fig.(ii)

4. Draw a line l at point A such that l is parallel to BC as shown in fig.(iii).
5. Draw any triangle KBC with the base BC and its vertex K lying on line l as shown in fig(iii).
6. Paste ΔEGH on △ ABC such that EH lies on BC and G does not lie on line l as shown in fig (iii).

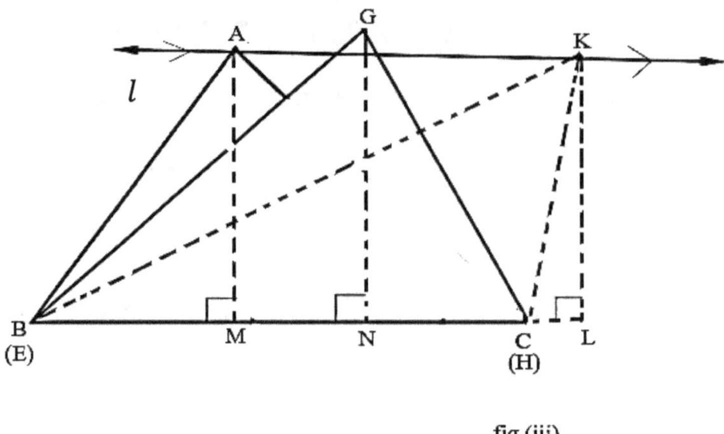

fig.(iii)

OBSERVATION

$$ar(\triangle ABC) = \frac{1}{2} \times \text{base} \times \text{height}$$

$$= \frac{1}{2} \times BC \times (\perp \text{ distance between } \parallel \text{ lines } l \text{ and } BC)$$

$$= \frac{1}{2} \times BC \times AM$$

$$ar(\triangle BKC) = \frac{1}{2} \times BC \times (\perp \text{distance between } \parallel \text{ lines } l \text{ and } BC)$$

$$= \frac{1}{2} \times BC \times KL$$

$$= \frac{1}{2} \times BC \times AM (\perp \text{ distance between } \parallel \text{ lines is always same }), (KL = AM)$$

$$\therefore \quad ar(\triangle ABC) = ar(\triangle BKC)$$

$$ar(\triangle EGH) = \frac{1}{2} \times \text{base} \times \text{height}$$

$$= \frac{1}{2} \times BC \times (\perp \text{ distance from G to BC})$$

$$= \frac{1}{2} \times BC \times GN$$

BUT, $\quad\quad\quad\quad AM \neq GN$

$\therefore \quad\quad\quad\quad ar(\triangle ABC) \neq ar(\triangle EGH)$

RESULT

We have verified that two triangles on the same base and between the same parallel lines are equal in area.

LEARNING OUTCOME

We learnt that areas of two or more triangles are same if they lie on the same base and between the same parallel lines. Triangles having same base but different perpendicular heights are not same and their areas are also not equal.

ACTIVITY TIME

Students can verify this theorem by graphical and counting methods.
[Hint: Draw two triangles on the same base and between the same height and then count the squares covered by two triangles on the graph paper].

Question 1. If two triangles are on the same base and between the same parallels, then what is the relationship between their areas?
Answer. Both triangles have equal area.

Question 2. If a student calculates the area of three triangles, which are drawn on the same base and between the same parallel lines. The areas calculated by him, different for third triangle. Does he, correct?
Answer. No, the area of all three triangles should be equal.

Question 3. If a triangle and a parallelogram are on the same base and between the same parallels, then what will be the relation in their areas?
Answer. Area of triangle will be half the area of the parallelogram.

Question 4. If two triangles lie on the same base and having equal areas. Will the triangles have equal altitudes?
Answer. Yes, triangles will have equal altitudes.

Question 5. If we draw infinite number of triangles on the same base and between the same parallel lines. Does the area of each triangle increase with increasing the distance from previous drawn triangle?
Answer. No, their areas will be same.

Question 6. What is the formula for the area of a triangle?
Answer. Area of a triangle is half the product of its base and the corresponding altitude.

MULTIPLE CHOICE QUESTION

Question 1.
In figure, if AE ∥ DC and AB = AC, find the value of $\angle ABD$.
(a) 130°
(b) 110°
(c) 120°
(d) 70°

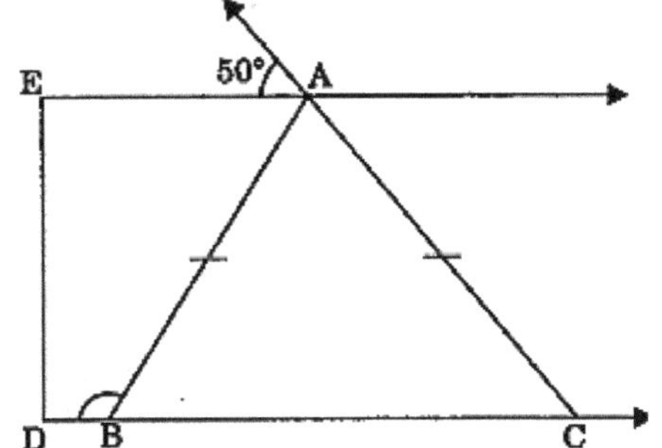

Question 2.
In triangles ABC and $PQR, AB = AC, \angle C = \angle P$ and $\angle B = \angle Q$. The two triangles are
(a) Isosceles but not congruent
(b) Isosceles and congruent
(c) Congruent but not isosceles
(d) Neither congruent nor isosceles

Question 3.
In the given figure, the measure of $\angle BAC$ is
(a) 60°
(b) 50°
(c) 70°
(d) 80°

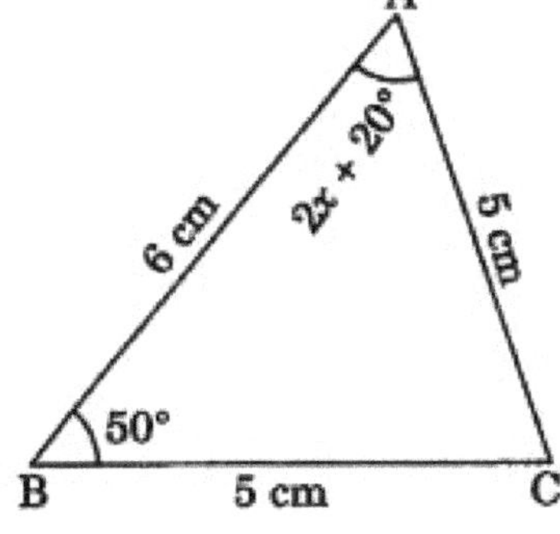

Question 4.
Two sides of a triangle are of lengths 5 cm and 1.5 cm. The length of the third side of the triangle cannot be:
(a) 3.6 cm
(b) 4.1 cm
(c) 3.8 cm
(d) 3.4 cm

Question 5.
For two triangles, if two angles and the included side of one triangle are equal to two angles and the included side of another triangle. Then the congruency rule is:
(a) SSS
(b) ASA
(c) SAS
(d) None of the above

Question 6.
In triangles ABC and PQR, AB = AC, $\angle C = \angle P$ and $\angle B = \angle Q$. The two triangles are
(a) Isosceles but not congruent
(b) Isosceles and congruent
(c) Congruent but not isosceles
(d) Neither congruent nor isosceles

Question 7.
In triangles ABC and DEF, AB = FD and $\angle A = \angle D$. The two triangles will be congruent by SAS axiom if
(a) BC = EF
(b) AC = DE
(c) AC = EF
(d) BC = DE

Question 8.
In triangles ABC and DEF, AB = FD and $\angle A = \angle D$. The two triangles will be congruent by SAS axiom if
(a) BC = EF
(b) AC = DE
(c) AC = EF
(d) BC = DE

Question 9.
In $\triangle$ ABC, $\angle C = \angle A$ and BC = 4 cm and AC = 5 cm, then find the length of AB.
(a) 5 cm
(b) 3 cm
(c) 4 cm
(d) 2.5 cm

Question 10.
In $\triangle$ ABC, AB = AC and $\angle B = 50°$, then find $\angle C$.
(a) 50°
(b) 40°
(c) 80°
(d) 120°

ANSWER KEY

| 1. (c) | 2. (d) | 3. (b) | 4. (a) | 5. (c) | 6. (d) | 7. (a) | 8. (b) | 9. (c) | 10. (a) |

ANGLE AT CENTRE IS DOUBLE THE ANGLE SUBTENDED BY SAME ARC AT ANY POINT ON CIRCUMFERENCE OF CIRCLE

OBJECTIVE
To verify that the angle subtended by an arc at the centre of the circle is double the angle subtended at any point on the remaining part of the circle, experimentally.

MATERIAL REQUIRED
Glazed papers, white sheet, pencil, a pair of scissors, glue stick.

THEORY
1. Basic terms related to a circle.
2. Concept of an angle subtended by an arc at the centre and the circumference of the circle.

PROCEDURE
1. Cut one circle of radius 2.5 cm with centre O from red coloured glazedpaper.
2. Cut three more circles from different coloured glazed papers of same radius.
3. Keep all four circles one on the other. Now fold along any part and press them to make a crease. On unfolding, we get chords of same length on each circle.
4. Name the chords, AB in the first circle with centre O.
5. Join OA and OB with pencil [fig. (i)].

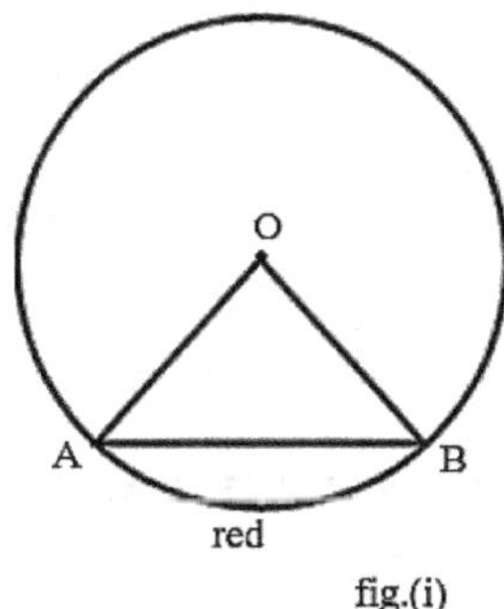

fig.(i)

6. Take two other circles of yellow and green colour and put one on the other and fold it such

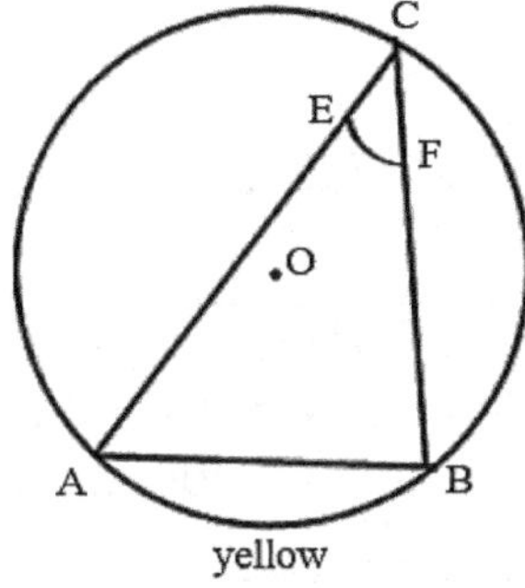

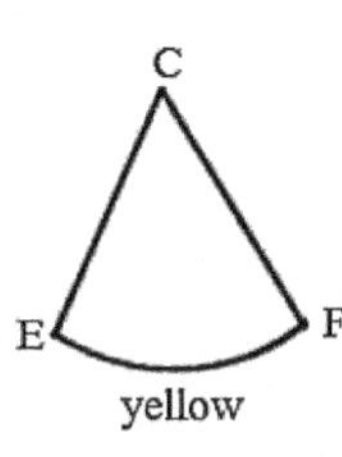

fig.(ii)

as to form an angle on the circumference with the same chord AB [fig. (ii) and (iii)].

7. Name these angles as ACB where AB is a chord.
8. Cut angles from fig. (ii) and (iii), ∠ACB from yellow circle and ∠ACB from green circle.
9. Cut the small portion of ∠ACB from both the circles [fig (ii) and (iii)].
10. Paste these two cut outs of fig. (ii) and (iii) on the other (blue) circle [fig. (iv)] at centre O such that their arms lie on the radius OA and OB of circle.

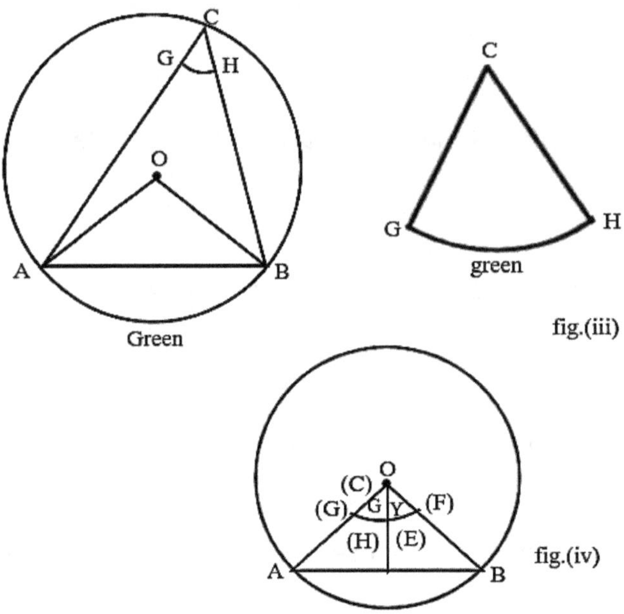

OBSERVATION

We observe that two cut outs of angles fully cover∠AOB in fig.(iv).

$$\angle AOB = \angle ECF + \angle GCH \text{ (as } \angle ECF = \angle GCH = \angle ACB)$$
$$= 2\angle ACB$$

RESULT

Hence, we verified that the angle subtended by an arc at the centre of circle is double the angle subtended by the same arc at any point on the remaining part of the circle.

LEARNING OUTCOME

Verification of the above theorem can be done for arc AB as major arc or semicircular arc. For semicircle, the angle on the diameter is 90°.

ACTIVITY TIME

To verify the converse of this theorem experimentally.

Question 1. Define a circle. **Answer:** A circle is the collection of all points in a plane that are equidistant from a fixed point within the same plane.	**Question 2.** What is a chord? **Answer:** A line segment is formed by joining any two points on the circumference of a circle.

Question 3. What will be the distance of two equal chords from the centre?
Answer: Both chords are at equal distance from the centre.

Question 4. What is the diameter?
Answer: The chord which passes through the centre of the circle is known as the diameter of circle.

Question 5. Which is the longest chord of a circle?
Answer: Diameter.

Question 6. If the angle subtended by an arc at the centre is 110°, then what will be the angle on the remaining part of the circle subtended by the same arc?
Answer: 55.

MULTIPLE CHOICE QUESTION

Question 1.
A regular octagon is inscribed in a circle. The angle that each side of the octagon subtends at the centre is:
(a) 45°
(b) 75°
(c) 90°
(d) 60°

Question 2.
Greatest chord of a circle is called its:
(a) Chord
(b) Secant
(c) Radius
(d) Diameter

Question 3 .
AD is the diameter of a circle and AB is a chord. If AD = 34 cm, AB = 30 cm, the distance of AB from the centre of the circle is
(a) 4 cm
(b) 8 cm
(c) 15 cm
(d) 17 cm

Question 4 .
A-line that intersects a circle in two distinct points is a:
(a) Secant
(b) Chord
(c) Radius
(d) Diameter

Question 5.
If chords AB and CD of congruent circles subtend equal angles at their centres, then:
(a) AB = CD
(b) AB > CD
(c) AB < AD
(d) None of the above

Question 6.
If there are two separate circles drawn apart from each other, then the maximum number of common points they have:
(a) 0
(b) 1
(c) 2
(d) 3

Question 7.
The angle subtended by the diameter of a semi-circle is:
(a) 90°
(b) 45°
(c) 180°
(d) 60°

Question 8.
The region between chord and either of the arc is called:
(a) A sector
(b) A semicircle
(c) A segment
(d) A quarter circles

<table>
<tr><td>

Question 9.
The region between an arc and the two radii joining the centre of the end points of the arc is called a:
(a) Segment
(b) Semi circle
(c) Minor arc
(d) Sector

</td><td>

Question 10.
The degree measure of a semicircle is:
(a) 0°
(b) 90°
(c) 360°
(d) 180°

</td></tr>
</table>

ANSWER KEY

| 1. (a) | 2. (d) | 3. (b) | 4. (a) | 5. (a) | 6. (a) | 7. (c) | 8. (c) | 9. (d) | 10. (d) |

ACTIVITY 24 — ANGLES IN THE SAME SEGMENT

OBJECTIVE
To show that the angles subtended by the chord of a circle in the same segment are equal, experimentally.

MATERIAL REQUIRED
Glazed papers, sketch pens, a pair of scissors, glue stick, geometry box, whitesheet.

THEORY
1. Concept of a circle.
2. Concept of the angle subtended by an arc/chord.

PROCEDURE
1. Take red colour glazed paper and draw a circle of any radius say 2.5 cm on the white side of the paper.
2. Cut this circle with centre O and radius 2.5 cm.
3. Mark any point P on the circumference of the circle.
4. Mark two other points A and B on the circumference of the circle.
5. Fold and press the circle along AB to get a crease which is a chord of the circle.
6. Join PA and PB to get $\angle APB$ as shown in fig.(i).

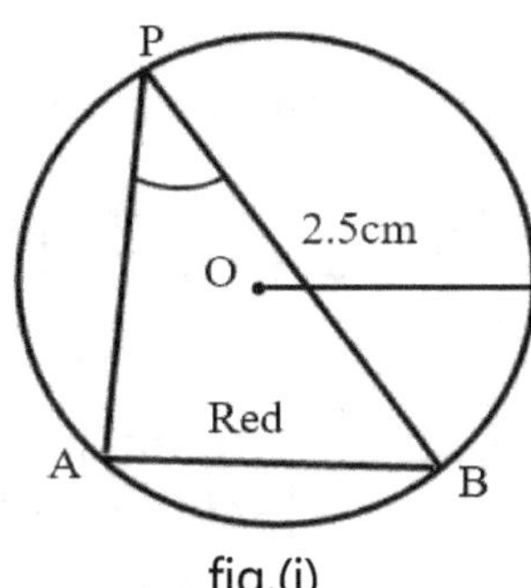

fig.(i)

7. Take another coloured glazed paper say, yellow, cut circle of same radius.
8. Draw a chord CD on the second circle with centre O', such that $AB = CD$.
9. Mark a point R on the circumference of the second circle. Join RC and RD fig (ii).

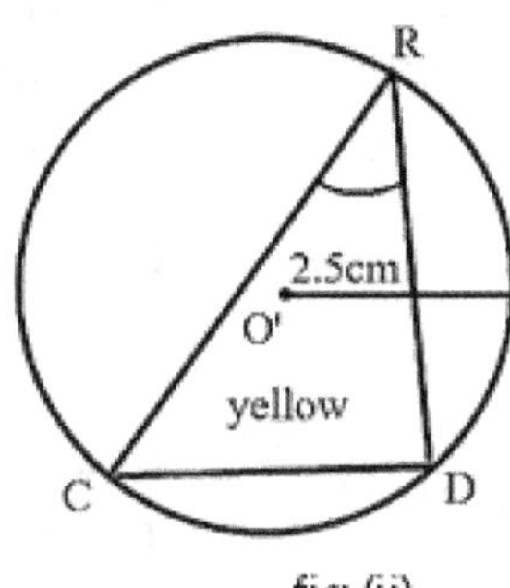

fig.(ii)

10. Cut out ΔRCD and paste it on the first circle such that R lies on P and RD lies on PB and RC lies on PA as shown in fig. (iii).

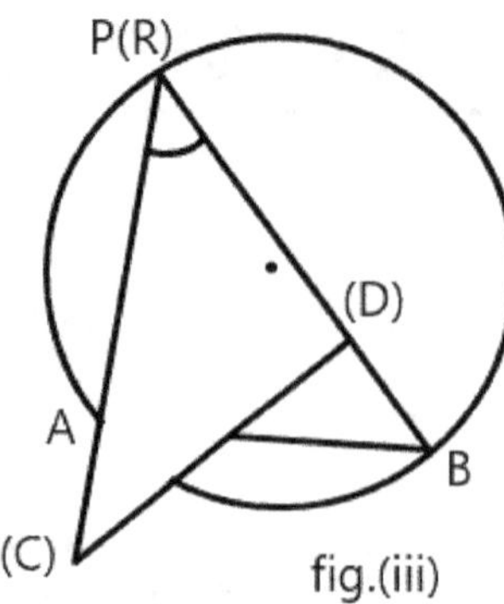

∠APB superimposes ∠DRC.

OBSERVATION

Since the chord AB = chord CD and ∠APB super imposes ∠DRC, their arcs are same. When two angles super impose each other, it means their two arms lie on one another. This verifies that angles in the same segments are equal.

RESULT

We verified that two angles subtended by the chord of a circle in the same segment are equal.

LEARNING OUTCOME

We learnt that two or more angles subtended by same chord in the same segment of a circle are equal.

ACTIVITY TIME

To verify experimentally that the angles in the same segment of a circle of radius 6 cm are equal.

Question 1. How will you relate the angles in the same segment of a circle? **Answer:** Angles will be equal.	**Question 4.** How will you define the major segment of a circle? **Answer.** A chord divides a circle into two parts and the larger part is called the major segment
Question 2. How many longest chords are there in a circle? **Answer:** There are infinite longest chords in a circle passing through the centre and each of them is equal to the diameter of the circle.	**Question 5.** Does equal chords of a circle subtend different angles at the centre? **Answer:** No, because equal chords subtended equal angles at the centre.
Question 3. What do you mean by the minor segment of a circle? **Answer:** A chord divides a circle into two parts and the smaller part is called the minor segment.	**Question 6.** The angle subtended by an arc at the circle in the minor segment is an obtuse angle. What is the value of the angle subtended by it in the major segment? **Answer:** Acute angle.

Question 7. If a chord AB subtended an angle 80° at centre, then what will be the measure of angles subtended by same chord in the same segment of the circle at points P and Q? **Answer:** Chord AB subtended an angle of 40° at both points.	**Question 8.** The line is drawn through the centre of a circle to bisect a chord is perpendicular to the chord. Is this statement true? **Answer:** Yes.

MULTIPLE CHOICE QUESTION

Question 1.
Any angle whose vertex is at the centre of the circle is called:
(a) Reflex angle
(b) Straight angle
(c) Central angle
(d) Right angle

Question 2.
If the angles subtended by the chords of a circle at the centre are equal, then the chords are:
(a) Not equal to each other
(b) Parallel to each other
(c) Equal to each other
(d) Perpendicular to each other

Question 3.
In a circle with centre O and a chord BC, points D and E lie on the same side of BC. Then, if $\angle BDC = 80°$, then $\angle BEC =$.
(a) 80°
(b) 20°
(c) 160°
(d) 40°

Question 4.
In a circle with centre O and a chord BC, the point D lies on the same side BC as O. If $\angle$ BOC = 50°, then $\angle BDC =$.
(a) 25°
(b) 100°
(c) 75°
(d) 150°

Question 5.
A regular octagon is inscribed in a circle. The angle that each side of the octagon subtends at the centre is:
(a) 45°
(b) 75°
(c) 90°
(d) 60°

Question 6.
An equilateral triangle ABC is inscribed in a circle with centre O. Angle BOC will be:
(a) 130°
(b) 150°
(c) 120°
(d) 180°

Question 7.
Chord AB subtends $\angle AOB = 60°$ at centre. If OA = 5 cm then the length of AB (in cm) is:
(a) 6 cm
(b) 5 cm
(c) 7 cm
(d) 8 cm

Question 8.
If chords AB and CD of congruent circles subtend equal angles at their center's, then:
(a) AB = CD
(b) AB > CD
(c) AB < AD
(d) None of the above

ANSWER KEY

1. (c)	2. (c)	3. (a)	4. (a)	5. (a)	6. (c)	7. (b)	8. (a)

ACTIVITY 25

OBJECTIVE

To verify that the opposite angles of a cyclic quadrilateral are supplementary by paper folding activity.

MATERIAL REQUIRED

White paper sheet, compass, glazed papers, pencil, a pair of scissors, gluestick.

THEORY

1. A quadrilateral whose all four vertices lies on the circle is known as cyclic quadrilateral.
2. Concept of opposite angles of a quadrilateral.
3. Concept of Supplementary angles.

PROCEDURE

1. Draw a circle of radius 2 cm on a white glazed paper with centre O.
2. Cut this circle with centre O and draw one more circle of same radius.
3. Take any four points A, B, C, D on the circumference of both the circles.
4. Join AB, BC, CD, DA by paper folding on both the circles.
5. We get a cyclic quadrilateral ABCD on both the circles [fig.(i) and fig.(ii)].Take ∠A and ∠C of blue colour and ∠B and ∠D of pink colour in both circles.

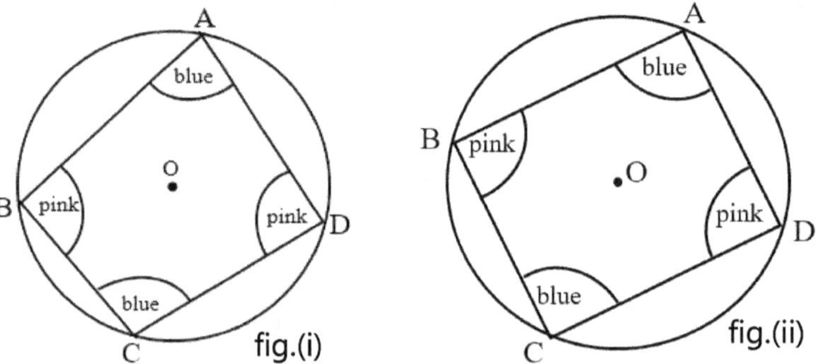

6. From the second circle, using transparent sheets makes cut outs of ∠A, ∠B, ∠C, ∠D. [fig.(iii)]. Take ∠A and ∠C of blue colour and ∠B and ∠D of pink colour.

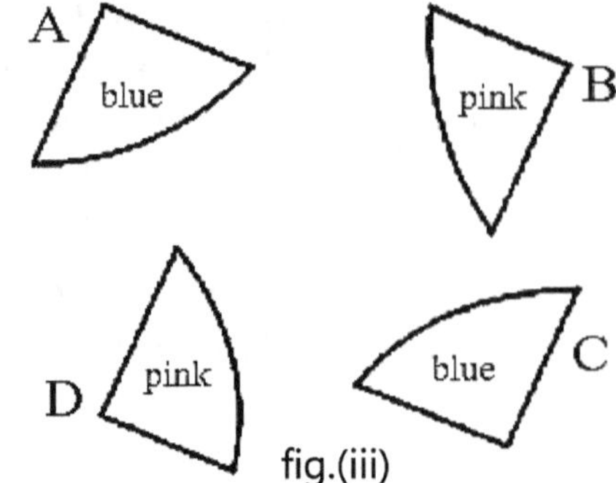

7. Make a straight line on a white paper sheet. Place cut outs of ∠A and ∠C adjacent to each other on a straight line and paste them [fig.(iv)].

8. Take cut outs of ∠B and ∠D and place them adjacent to each other on another straight line and paste them [fig.(iv)].

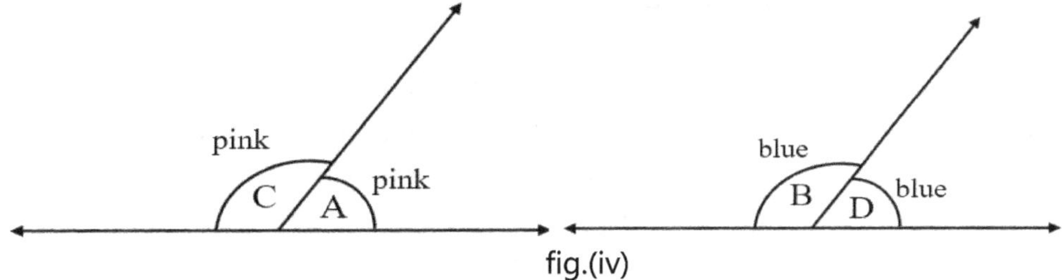

fig.(iv)

OBSERVATION

As ∠A and ∠C forms a linear pair.

∴ $\qquad \angle A + \angle C = 180°$

Similarly, $\qquad \angle B + \angle D = 180°$

RESULT

Hence, it is verified that in a cyclic quadrilateral, the sum of opposite angles is 180°.

LEARNING OUTCOME

If a cyclic quadrilateral is a parallelogram, then it becomes a rectangle, this can be proved by the paper folding and cutting method.

ACTIVITY TIME

Verify that the exterior angle of a cyclic quadrilateral is equal to the opposite interior angle.

VIVA-VOCE

Question 1. What do you understand by the term a cyclic quadrilateral?
Answer: A quadrilateral having all the vertices on the boundary of the circle is called a cyclic quadrilateral.

Question 2. What is the type of quadrilateral formed by the internal angle bisectors of cyclic quadrilateral?
Answer: Cyclic quadrilateral.

Question 3. If one of the angles of a cyclic quadrilateral is 40°, then what will be the value of its opposite angle?
Answer: 140°

Question 4. If a cyclic quadrilateral is a parallelogram, then what is the type of parallelogram?
Answer: Rectangle.

Question 5. Is the sum of adjacent angles of a cyclic quadrilateral 180° ?
Answer: No, only the sum of opposite angles of a cyclic quadrilateral is 180°.

Question 6. What is the name of quadrilateral if each pair of opposite angles is supplementary?
Answer: Cyclic quadrilateral.

Question 7. Which property has to be added in a trapezium for making it a cyclic quadrilateral?
Answer: Non-parallel sides of a trapezium should be equal.

Question 8. What is the sum of each pair of opposite angles of a cyclic quadrilateral?
Answer: 180°

Question 1.
ABCD is a cyclic quadrilateral in which AC and BD are its diagonals. If $\angle DBC = 59°$ and $\angle BAC = 45°$, then $\angle BCD = $.
(a) 60°
(b) 70°
(c) 76°
(d) 75°

Question 2.
ABCD is a cyclic quadrilateral in which AC and BD are its diagonals. If $\angle DBC = 50°$ and $\angle BAC = 40°$, then $\angle BCD = $
(a) 60°
(b) 90°
(c) 75°
(d) 80°

Question 3.
Find the value of x if ABCD is a cyclic quadrilateral if $\angle 1 : \angle 2 = 3 : 6$.
(a) 90°
(b) 45°
(c) 60°
(d) 20°

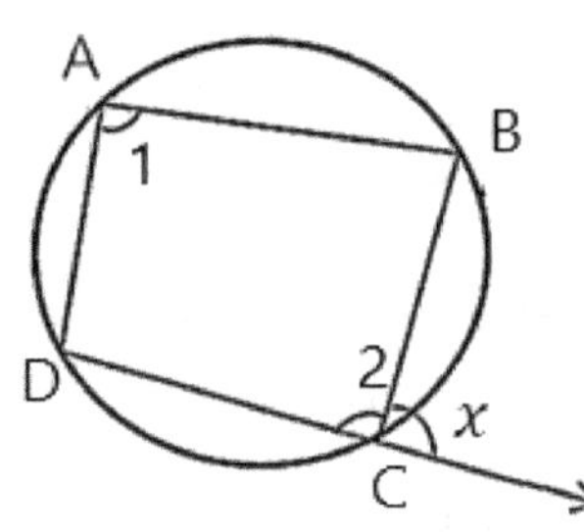

Question 4.
What is the value of $\angle PRQ$ if $\angle PSR : \angle PQR = 1 : 2$?

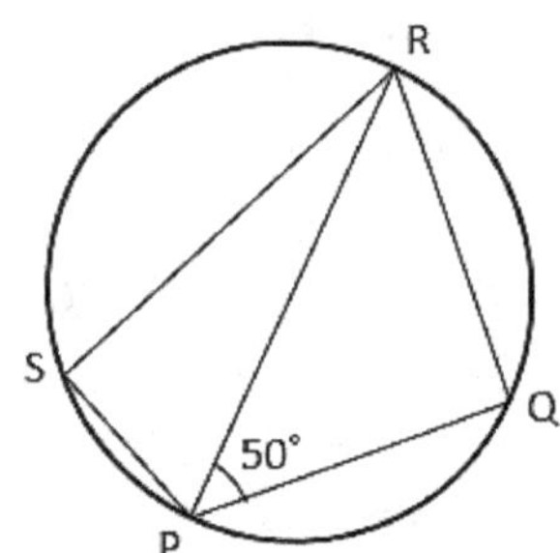

(a) 50°
(b) 10°
(c) 90°
(d) 45°

Question 5.
What is the value of $\angle PQR$ if PQRS is cyclic quadrilateral and PS = SR?
(a) 90°
(b) 70°
(c) 40°
(d) 30°

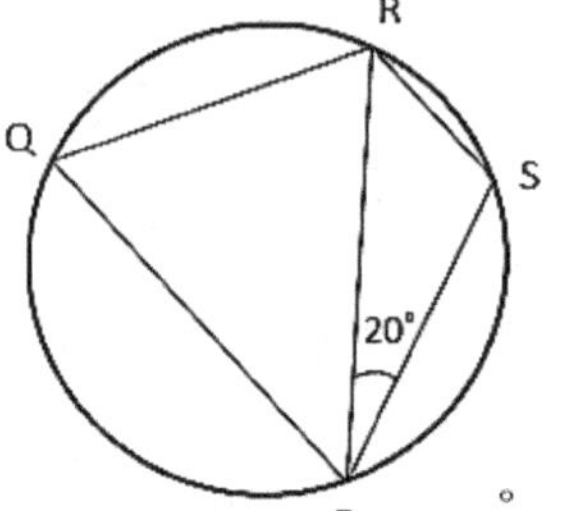

Question 6.
Find the value of $\angle PQR$ if $PS \parallel RQ$ and $PQRS$ is cyclic quadrilateral.

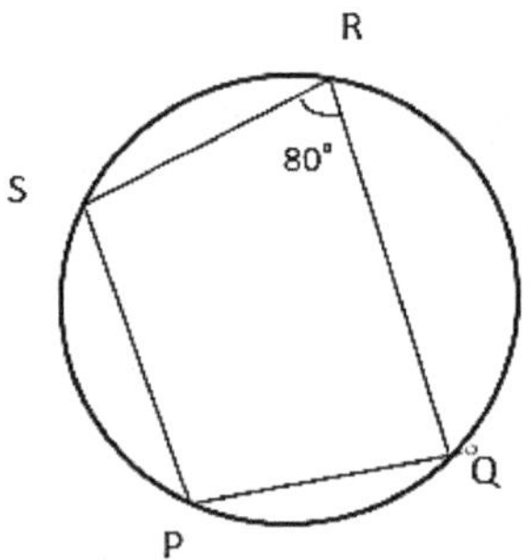

(a) 45°
(b) 50°
(c) 80°
(d) 90°

Question 7.
ABCD is a cyclic trapezium in which $AD \parallel BC$, if $\angle B = 70°$, find the value of $\angle A$:
(a) 70°
(b) 110°
(c) 35°
(d) None of these

Question 8.
If ABCD is a cyclic quadrilateral, in which $\angle DBC = 70°$, $\angle BAC = 40°$, find $\angle BCD$:
(a) 100°
(b) 40°
(c) 70°
(d) None of these

Question 9.	**Question 10.**

Question 9.
ABCD is a cyclic quadrilateral. Side CD is produced on both sides such that $\angle BCP = 110°$, the value of $\angle A$ is:
(a) 100°
(b) 110°
(c) 80°
(d) None of these

Question 10.
Find the value of x and y if ABCD is cyclic quadrilateral.
(a) 60°, 60°
(b) 50°, 60°
(c) 45°, 45°
(d) 80°, 90°

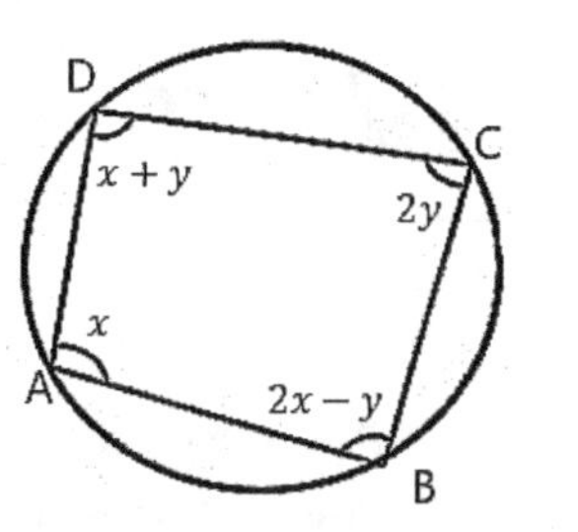

ANSWER KEY

1.(c)	2.(b)	3.(d)	4.(b)	5.(c)	6.(a)	7.(b)	8.(c)	9.(c)	10.(a)

ANGLE IN A SEMICIRCLE, MAJOR SEGMENT, MINOR SEGMENT

OBJECTIVE

To verify that angle in a semicircle is a right angle, angle in a major segment is acute, angle in a minor segment is obtuse by paper folding.

MATERIAL REQUIRED

White sheet, glazed papers, compass, pencil, tracing paper

THEORY

1. Concept of a semicircle, major segment and minor segments
2. Concept of right angle, acute angle and obtuse angle.

PROCEDURE

CASE I.

1. Draw a circle of any radius with centre O on a glazed paper. Cut it and paste it on white paper.
2. Fold the circle along the line passing through the centre O to get a diameter AB.
3. Take any point P on the circumference of the circle.
4. Join AP and BP by paper folding to get $\angle APB$.
5. Make two replicas of $\angle APB$ with the help of tracing paper such that $\angle A_1 P_1 B_1$ and $\angle A_2 P_2 B_2$.

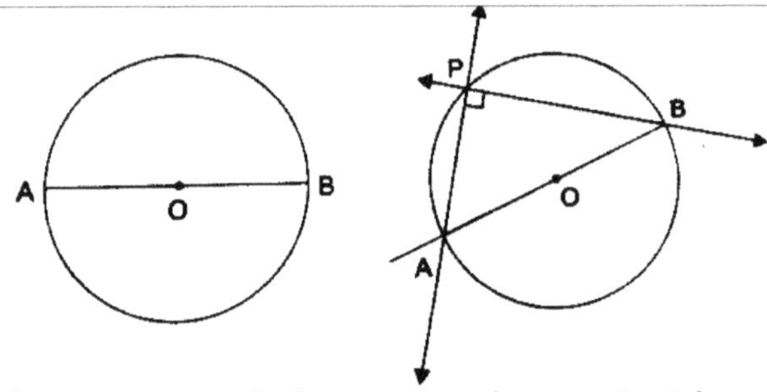

6. Place two $\Delta A_1 P_1 B_1$ and $\Delta A_2 P_2 B_2$ such that $\angle P_1$ and $\angle P_2$ coincide each other fig.(ii).

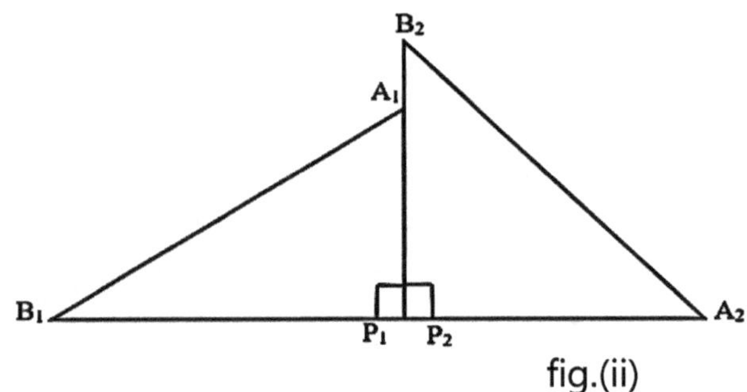

fig.(ii)

We notice $\angle A_1 P_1 B_1$ and $\angle A_2 P_2 B_2$ form a linear pair.

$$\therefore \quad \angle A_1 P_1 B_1 + \angle A_2 P_2 B_2 = 180° \quad \text{(Linear pair).}$$
$$2\angle APB = 180° \quad (\angle A_1 P_1 B_1 \text{and} \angle A_2 P_2 B_2 \text{ are replicas of } \angle APB)$$
$$\therefore \quad \angle APB = 90°$$

CASE II.

FOR MAJOR SEGMENT:

1. Cut a circle of any radius using glazed paper with centre O and paste it on white paper.
2. Make a chord AB by paper folding.
3. Take a point Q on the major segment. Join QA and QB by paper folding.

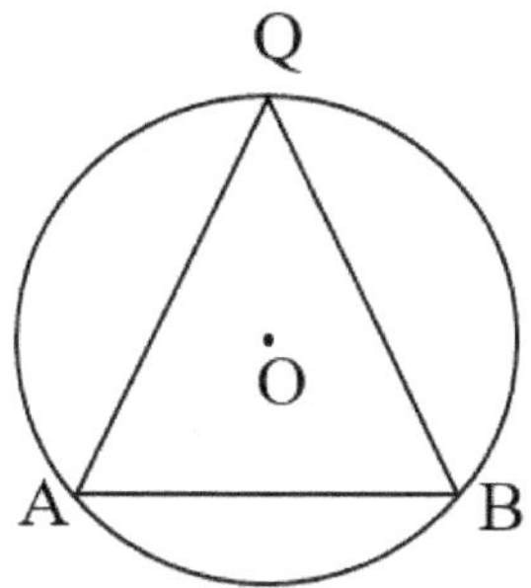

4. Draw and cut replica of $\angle$AQB.
5. Place the replica of $\angle$AQB on the newly drawn, right-angled ΔDEF such that side BQ falls on DE.

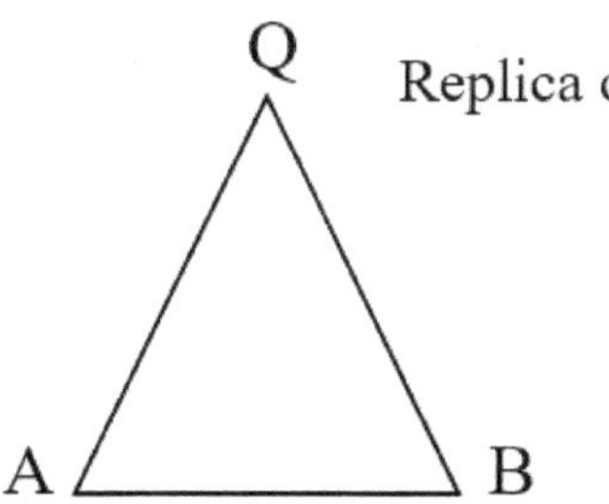

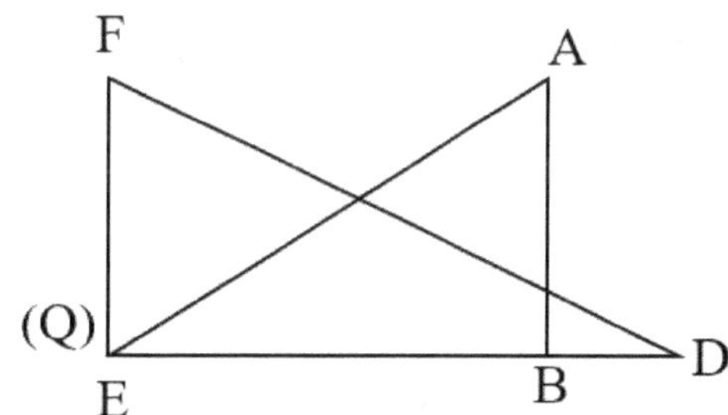

$$\therefore \qquad \angle AQB < \angle DEF = 90°$$
$$\therefore \qquad \angle AQB \text{ is acute.}$$

CASE III.

FOR MINOR SEGMENT:

1. Cut a circle of any radius using glazed paper with centre O. Paste it on white paper.
2. Make a chord AB by paper folding.
3. Take any point M on the minor segment. Join MA and MB by paper folding to get $\angle$AMB.
4. Draw and cut replica of $\angle$AMB with the help of tracing paper.
5. Place the replica of $\angle$AMB on the base of the newly drawn right angled triangle ΔDEF, such that base MB coincides with EF and point M coincides with E.

Here, $\qquad \angle AMB > \angle DEF = 90°$

$\therefore \qquad \angle AMB$ is an obtuse angle.

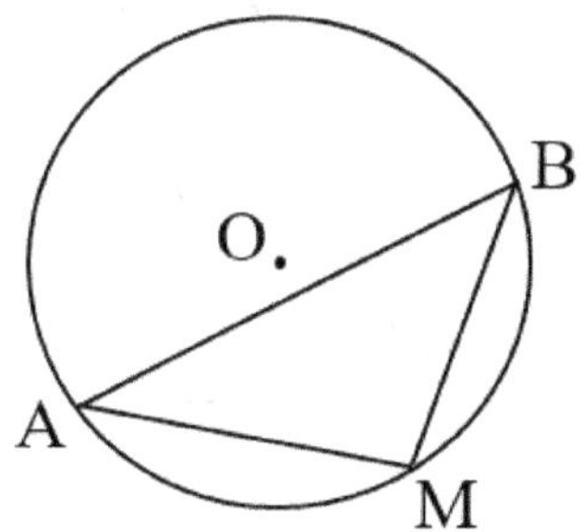

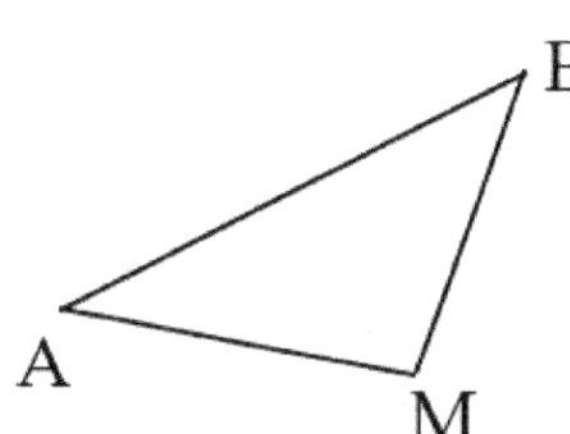

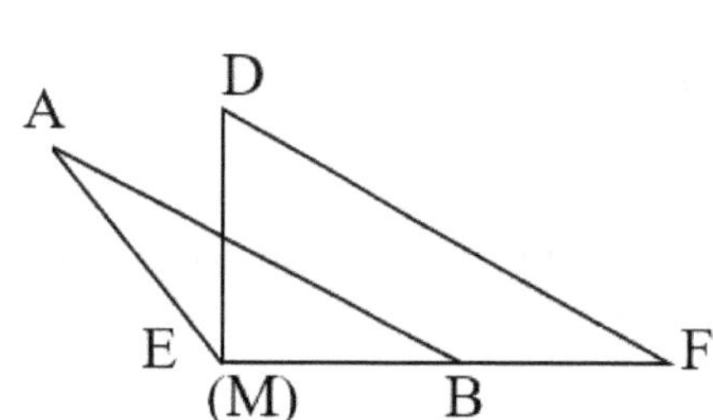

OBSERVATION

We observe that
In Case I, AOB is diameter and ∠APB is 90°.
In Case II, AQB is a major segment and ∠AQB is an acute angle.
In Case III, AMB is a minor segment and ∠AMB is an obtuse angle.

RESULT

By paper folding method, we verified that angle in a semicircle is a right angle. In any circle, the angle in the minor segment is an obtuse angle, angle in the major segment is an acute angle.

LEARNING OUTCOME

In any circle, any angle in a minor segment is always obtuse, any angle in a major segment is always acute, angle in a semicircle is always a right angle.

ACTIVITY TIME

Divide the circle into two parts:
1. Along the diameter and measure different angles formed on the diameter by the paper folding method.
2. Along any chord (other than diameter) and measure the different angles formed by paper folding on two different segments.

VIVA-VOCE

Question 1: The line is drawn through the centre of a circle to bisect a chord is perpendicular to the chord". Is this statement true?
Answer: Yes

Question 2: How many longest chords are there in a circle?
Answer: There are infinite longest chords in a circle passing through the centre and each of them is equal to the diameter of the circle.

Question 3: What do you mean by the minor segment of a circle?
Answer: A chord divides a circle into two parts and the smaller part is called the minor segment.

Question 4: How will you define the major segment of a circle?
Answer: A chord divides a circle into two parts and the larger part is called the major segment.

Question 5: Does equal chords of a circle subtend different angles at the centre?
Answer: No, because equal chords subtended equal angles at the centre.

Question 6: The angle subtended by an arc at the circle in the minor segment is an obtuse angle. What is the value of angle subtended by it in the major segment?
Answer: Acute angle

Question 7: If a chord AB subtended an angle 80° at the centre, then what will be the measure of angles subtended by same chord in the same segment of the circle at points P and Q?
Answer: Chord AB subtended an angle of 40° at both points.

Question 8: How will you relate the angles in the same segment of a circle?
Answer: Angles will be equal.

$$\boxed{\textbf{MULTIPLE CHOICE QUESTION}}$$

Question 1.
If the circumference of a circle is 22 cm, find the area of the semicircle.
(a) 38.5 cm²
(b) 19.25 cm²
(c) 44 cm²
(d) 77 cm²

Question 2.
The angle subtended by the diameter of a semicircle is:
(a) 45°
(b) 180°
(c) 90°
(d) 60°

Question 3.
The area of a sector of a circle is $\frac{1}{6}$ to the area of the circle. Find the degree measure of its minor arc.
(a) 90°
(b) 60°
(c) 45°
(d) 30°

Question 4.
If there are two separate circles drawn apart from each other, then the maximum number of common points they have:
(a) 0
(b) 1
(c) 2
(d) 3

Question 5.
Equal _____ of the congruent circles subtend equal angles at the centres.
(a) Segments
(b) Radii
(c) Arcs
(d) Chords

Question 6.
If chords AB and CD of congruent circles subtend equal angles at their centres, then:
(a) AB = CD
(b) AB > CD
(c) AB < AD
(d) None of the above

Question 7.
Equal _____ of the congruent circles subtend equal angles at the centres.
(a) Segments
(b) Radii
(c) Arcs
(d) Chords

Question 8.
Find the area of a right-angled triangle, if the radius of its circumcircle is 3 cm and altitude drawn to the hypotenuse is 2 cm:
(a) 3 cm²
(b) 6 cm²
(c) 2 cm²
(d) None of these

Question 9.
If the angle in major segment is acute, then angle opposite to it will be:
(a) Obtuse
(b) Right angle
(c) Acute
(d) None of these

Question 10.
If the angle in minor segment is obtuse then other angle on the same segment will be:
(a) Right angle
(b) Acute
(c) Obtuse
(d) None of these

ANSWER KEY

1.(b)	2.(c)	3.(b)	4.(a)	5.(d)	6.(a)	7.(d)	8.(b)	9.(a)	10.(c)

Experiment No. ....   Date. ....

Remarks....................   Teacher's Signature ....

Experiment No. ....   Date. ....

Remarks.....................   Teacher's Signature ....

Experiment No. ....   Date. ....

Remarks......................   Teacher's Signature ....

Experiment No. ....   Date. ....

Remarks......................   Teacher's Signature ....

Experiment No. ....   Date. ....

Remarks.....................   Teacher's Signature ....

Experiment No. ....   Date. ....

Remarks.....................   Teacher's Signature ....

Experiment No. ....   Date. ....

Remarks.....................   Teacher's Signature ....

Experiment No. ....   Date. ....

Remarks.....................   Teacher's Signature ....

Experiment No. ....   Date. ....

Remarks.....................   Teacher's Signature ....

Experiment No. ....   Date. ....

Remarks.....................   Teacher's Signature ....

Experiment No. ....   Date. ....

Remarks.....................   Teacher's Signature ....

Experiment No. ....   Date. ....

Remarks.....................   Teacher's Signature ....

Experiment No. ....

Date. ....

Remarks....................

Teacher's Signature ....

Experiment No. ....   Date. ....

Remarks.....................   Teacher's Signature ....

Experiment No. ....   Date. ....

Remarks.....................   Teacher's Signature ....

Experiment No. ....   Date. ....

Remarks.....................   Teacher's Signature ....

Experiment No. ....   Date. ....

Remarks......................   Teacher's Signature ....

Experiment No. ....   Date. ....

Remarks......................   Teacher's Signature ....

Experiment No. ....   Date. ....

Remarks......................   Teacher's Signature ....

Experiment No. ....   Date. ....

Remarks.....................   Teacher's Signature ....

Experiment No. ....   Date. ....

Remarks.....................   Teacher's Signature ....

Experiment No. ....   Date. ....

Remarks....................   Teacher's Signature ....

Experiment No. ....   Date. ....

Remarks.....................   Teacher's Signature ....

Experiment No. ....   Date. ....

Remarks....................   Teacher's Signature ....

Experiment No. ....   Date. ....

Remarks.....................   Teacher's Signature ....

Experiment No. ....   Date. ....

Remarks.....................   Teacher's Signature ....

Experiment No. ....   Date. ....

Remarks......................   Teacher's Signature ....

Experiment No. ....   Date. ....

Remarks.....................   Teacher's Signature ....

Experiment No. ....   Date. ....

Remarks.....................   Teacher's Signature ....

Experiment No. ....   Date. ....

Remarks.....................   Teacher's Signature ....

Experiment No. ....   Date. ....

Remarks.....................   Teacher's Signature ....

Experiment No. ....   Date. ....

Remarks.....................   Teacher's Signature ....

Experiment No. ....   Date. ....

Remarks.....................   Teacher's Signature ....

Experiment No. ....   Date. ....

Remarks.....................   Teacher's Signature ....

Experiment No. ....   Date. ....

Remarks......................   Teacher's Signature ....

Experiment No. ....   Date. ....

Remarks...................   Teacher's Signature ....

Experiment No. ....   Date. ....

Remarks.....................   Teacher's Signature ....

Experiment No. ....   Date. ....

Remarks.....................   Teacher's Signature ....

Experiment No. ....   Date. ....

Remarks.....................   Teacher's Signature ....

Experiment No. ....   Date. ....

Remarks.....................   Teacher's Signature ....

Experiment No. ....   Date. ....

Remarks......................   Teacher's Signature ....

Experiment No. ....   Date. ....

Remarks.....................   Teacher's Signature ....

Experiment No. ....   Date. ....

Remarks.....................   Teacher's Signature ....

Experiment No. ....   Date. ....

Remarks.....................   Teacher's Signature ....

9 789355 563446